The Liturgy of the World:

Karl Rahner's
Theology of Worship

Michael Skelley, S.J.

The Liturgy of the World:

Karl Rahner's
Theology of Worship

Foreword by

Rembert G. Weakland, O.S.B.

Archbishop of Milwaukee

A PUEBLO BOOK

The Liturgical Press   Collegeville, Minnesota

A Pueblo book published by The Liturgical Press

Design by Frank Kacmarcik

Library of Congress Cataloging-in-Publication Data

Skelley, Michael.
  The liturgy of the world : Karl Rahner's theology of worship /
Michael Skelley ; foreword by Rembert G. Weakland.
  p.   cm.
Includes bibliographical references.
ISBN 0-8146-6009-6
1. Rahner, Karl, 1904–   . 2. Man (Christian theology)
3. Catholic Church—Doctrines. I. Title.
BX4705.R287S55 1991
248.3'092—dc20   91-12953
                                                            CIP

To my mother and father,

        my first teachers
        in the faith

Contents

Foreword

In his advice to the cellarer of the monastery, Benedict, in chapter 32 of his *Rule* for monks, states that the person chosen by the abbot should "regard all the utensils and goods of the monastery as sacred vessels of the altar." In a very real and simple way Benedict ties together prayer and work, the sacred and the secular. Monastic tradition was much influenced by this closing of the dichotomy between liturgy and life, the dualism of sacred and profane that had so often plagued Christianity since early times.

Karl Rahner was aware of this same question in our own day, a question probably in fact having become even more exacerbated by our more scientific approach to the secular and to nature. The experiential question of how life relates to liturgy is one that affects how one views ultimately the way God relates to this world. Rahner was able, then, to look at liturgy in the light of his whole approach to the relationship between the divine and the human. His reflections have had a strong impact on our present thinking about sacraments, liturgy, life, God, and us.

The transcendent is not limited to the liturgy; there are other ways in which God relates to us humans. Rahner knew this almost instinctively and then set about to try to bring all these experiences of the transcendent into a logical broad picture. Because he was asking the right question, his answer is most important to us today.

First of all, it is imperative that we interpret Rahner rightly and not through some of the popularizations of his concepts. In this respect this work by Father Skelley is most useful to all of us. Rahner is often not easy to read; he presupposes that one has followed his theological journey over the years. His terminology can be confusing; his long sentences can be distracting. It is good to have a clear review of his important teaching on this issue and a proper understanding of his starting points.

In some respects Rahner goes beyond Pope Paul VI's famous passage in *Mysterium fidei* where the Pope talks about the different but real presences of Christ in the Church. Finally, Pope Paul leads this discussion to the special and real presence of Christ in the Eucharist (September 3, 1965, par. 35) without denying the other presences or their realness. Rahner talks about the real presence of God in the world—the liturgy of the world—and leads up to the liturgy as we know it. Rahner knows that the transcendent is not limited to the liturgy as we know it and that God acts in the world. But the precise question of how all the divine manifestations are tied together and find their symbolic representation in the liturgy has not been better answered by anyone before Rahner's time.

It is unfortunate, perhaps, that his writings have often been presented in such a way as almost to deny the need for sacraments and liturgy. Such presentations, in their simplified and often falsified form, have crept into our catechetical texts. It is good that the full and correct concept of Rahner in all his rigor and breadth is presented here. Rahner would be horrified if he thought that his theological explanation was being used to deny the very need for liturgy and sacraments, as if they were unnecessary adjuncts to life, ones that one could just as well do without.

It is a loss to us that Rahner did not answer some of the other interesting questions that can arise from his thesis. How does the liturgical experience affect one's life experience of God? How does the aesthetic experience affect one's liturgical and life experience of God? These and many other questions suggest themselves. Perhaps the one question that we wish he had written more extensively on would have been the unique contribution of the liturgical experience for the whole of one's spirituality. Nevertheless, he has given us enough of a basis for pursuing these areas and for expanding his ideas.

This work by Father Skelley will open up more questions and lead to more answers that unify our experiences of God. I hope it will also be the basis for deeper reflections on the oneness of

God's work among us in its many different colors. Most of all, I would hope that this expanded vision would open up our eyes to the liturgy of the world around us and make us sensitive to God's action in our lives and in the events of our times. The best contributions to theological reflection we know are not always those that answer all our questions but rather those that lead us to a deeper analysis of our life experiences. Rahner has done just that for liturgy and life.

Rembert G. Weakland, O.S.B.
Archbishop of Milwaukee

Abbreviations

KuD	*Kerygma und Dogma*
FZPhTh	*Freiburger Zeitschrift für Philosophie und Theologie*
PCTSA	Proceedings of the Catholic Theological Society of America
STh	*Schriften zur Theologie*
TD	*Theology Digest*
ThGl	*Theologie und Glaube*
TI	*Theological Investigations*
TS	*Theological Studies*
ZKTh	*Zeitschrift für Katholische Theologie*
ZThK	*Zeitschrift für Theologie und Kirche*

Introduction

Karl Rahner, S.J. (1904–1984), has clearly been one of the most important and influential theologians of this century. When he was asked in 1982 to sum up what he hoped to accomplish through his theological work, he replied:

"I would plainly and simply say that I am a Catholic Christian, I am attempting to reflect on my faith and relate it to the questions, needs, and difficulties, which confront me as a man and a Christian. From this everything else follows. Of course, I pursued one thing or another in scholarly theology in the strict sense and in historical theology—this follows from my office as professor. But in general, I really have endeavored to pursue a theology that looks to concrete proclamation in the Church, to dialogue with people of today. Perhaps some will believe that this is just the opposite of what I have done, for there are, of course, many people who say that my writings are not understandable, that I write sentences that are too long, and so on. I believe, however, that the pastoral concern of proclaiming the Christian faith for today has been the normative aspect of my work."[1]

1. Karl Rahner, "I am a Priest and a Theologian," *Karl Rahner in Dialogue: Conversations and Interviews, 1965–1982*, ed. P. Imhof and H. Biallowons, trans. ed. H. Egan (New York: Crossroad, 1986) 334. For further information on Karl Rahner's life and theological activity, *see* Karl Rahner, *I Remember: An Autobiographical Interview with Meinold Krauss*, trans. H. Egan (New York: Crossroad, 1985); Herbert Vorgrimler, *Understanding Karl Rahner: An Introduction to His Life and Thought* (New York: Crossroad, 1986); Paul Imhof und Hubert Biallowons, hrsg., *Karl Rahner: Bilder eines Lebens* (Köln: Benziger, 1985); and Karl-Heinz Weger, *Karl Rahner: An Introduction to His Theology* (New York: Seabury, 1980). For an American assessment of Rahner *see* William Dych, "The Achievement of Karl Rahner," TD 31 (1984) 325–333; Michael Fahey, "1904–1984, Karl Rahner, Theologian," PCTSA 39 (1984)

In this modest fashion, Rahner summarized a lifetime of theological ministry through which he had an enormous impact on the Christian community. He struggled with all the resources of his heart and mind to respond to the questions of his age and the needs of the Church he loved. In the process he opened up a profound, new understanding of what it means to be Christian in the modern world. Johann Baptist Metz expressed Rahner's influence well when he said: "Karl Rahner has renewed the face of our theology. Nothing is quite as it was before him. Even those who criticize him or reject him still live on his insights, his acute and sensitive perceptions in the world of life and faith."[2]

An issue that took on new urgency during Rahner's lifetime was the need to revitalize the Church's worship. The liturgical movement had begun early in the nineteenth century and became increasingly influential in the 1940s and 1950s. This movement provided the Church with a wealth of pastoral experience in the renewal of its worship. Simultaneously, scholars in a variety of theological disciplines returned to their sources and gained new insights into the Christian liturgical traditions. These developments came to fruition when the Second Vatican Council issued a constitution on the renewal of the liturgy, *Sacrosanctum concilium*, as its first decree.[3] Ever since, the whole Christian community has been working to renew its theology and practice of worship. Rahner's theology was always attuned to concrete pastoral questions, and so it is not surprising that he, too, would have turned his attention to the renewal of the Church's liturgical life.

84-98; and Leo O'Donovan, "A Journey into Time: The Legacy of Karl Rahner's Last Years," TS 46 (1985) 621-646.

2. Quoted in H. Vorgrimler, *Understanding Karl Rahner*, ix.

3. For a brief summary of the liturgical movement, see H. Ellsworth Chandlee, "The Liturgical Movement," *The New Westminster Dictionary of Liturgy and Worship*, ed. J. G. Davies (Philadelphia: Westminster Press, 1986) 307-314. For the context and process of *Sacrosanctum concilium*, see Fredrick R. McManus, "The Sacred Liturgy: Tradition and Change," *Remembering the Future: Vatican II and Tomorrow's Liturgical Agenda*, ed. C. Last (New York: Paulist, 1983) 11-32.

Rahner took an interest in the theology of worship very early in his career. He wrote extensively on topics such as the sacraments, the celebration of the Eucharist, and the relationship between the Church and the sacraments. Of all the theological topics that he addressed in his long career, the only one in which he was sufficiently interested to do extensive historical research was a topic in sacramental theology: penance in the early Church. The entire span of his writings is laced with observations on worship. Even when Rahner did not make explicit mention of liturgy or sacraments, his theology is often implicitly related to the theology of worship. Any reader with even a casual interest in the theology of worship cannot help but notice that Rahner's vision of the faith offers a new and deeper understanding of the Church's liturgical life.[4]

Rahner's theology of worship should be understood in the context of his lifelong theological project. He claims that between the simple repetition of traditional catechetical formulas on the one hand and the process of mastering all the theological disciplines on the other, there is a way of giving an intellectually honest justification of Christian faith on what he calls "the first level of reflection." Such a justification of the faith has to be possible because even a professional theologian can only be competent in one or two of the many disciplines involved in scholarly theol-

4. Rahner developed the main features of his liturgical theology in an article published in 1979 entitled "On the Theology of Worship." Originally published as "Zur Theologie des Gottesdienstes" in *Tübinger Theologische Quartalschrift* 159 (1979) 162-169; it was republished in Karl Rahner, STh 14 (Einsiedeln: Benziger, 1980) 227-237, and translated into English in Karl Rahner, TI 19 (New York: Crossroad, 1983) 141-149. That article builds closely on one he originally published in 1970 entitled "Considerations on the Active Role of the Person in the Sacramental Event." Originally published as "Überlegungen zum personalen Vollzug des sakramentalen Geschehens" in *Geist und Leben* 43 (1970) 282-301 and in *Frau und Mutter* (Düsseldorf, 1970) 262-264, 303-305, 361-362; it was republished in STh 10 (Einsiedeln: Benziger, 1972) 405-429; and translated into English in TI 14 (New York: Seabury, 1976) 161-184. These articles capture in a unique fashion Rahner's insights into the liturgical life of the Church. *See* Michael Skelley, "The Liturgy of the World and the Liturgy of the Church: Karl Rahner's Idea of Worship," *Worship* 63 (1989) 112-132.

ogy. None of us could live our faith with real intellectual integrity and honesty if we had to answer all the questions of professional theologians. The various disciplines of academic theology are vitally important, but they constitute a second level of reflection beyond that required for an intellectually honest faith.[5]

Since neither theologians nor their readers can master all the relevant intellectual disciplines, they need not be expected to do so. It is possible to give a justification of the faith without entering into all the questions or adopting all the methods of contemporary intellectual enquiry. Such a justification of the faith on the first level of reflection does not excuse one from striving toward the highest intellectual standards. It simply operates on the assumption that it is not necessary to answer every possible question in order to have a reasonable faith. The vast majority of Rahner's theological writings, difficult and demanding as they may be, are intended by him to be such first-level reflections. For example, his *Foundations of Christian Faith: An Introduction to the Idea of Christianity* is one such first-level reflection on the idea of Christianity and not a complete systematic theology.

Rahner readily admits that there are many important issues concerning the idea of worship that he has not treated.[6] But it is impossible for any theologian today to produce singlehandedly a theology of worship that would completely and rigorously ad-

5. Karl Rahner, *Foundations of Christian Faith: An Introduction to the Idea of Christianity* (New York: Seabury, 1978) 8–10. For a detailed exposition of his theological method *see* Karl Rahner, "Reflections on Methodology in Theology," TI 11 (New York: Crossroad, 1982) 68–114; and "Transcendental Theology," *Encyclopedia of Theology: The Concise* Sacramentum Mundi, ed. K. Rahner (New York: Crossroad, 1982) 1748–1751. *See also* Otto Much, *The Transcendental Method* (New York: Herder and Herder, 1968); Anne Carr, *The Theological Method of Karl Rahner* (Missoula: Scholar's Press, 1977); William V. Dych, "Method in Theology According to Karl Rahner," *Theology and Discovery: Essays in Honor of Karl Rahner, S.J.*, ed. W. J. Kelly (Milwaukee: Marquette University Press, 1980) 39–53; Gerald A. McCool, "The Philosophical Theology of Rahner and Lonergan," *God Knowable and Unknowable*, ed. R. J. Roth (New York: Fordham University Press, 1973) 123–157; and Leo O'Donovan, "Orthopraxis and Theological Method in Karl Rahner," PCTSA 35 (1980) 47–65.

6. K. Rahner, "On the Theology of Worship," 145–148.

dress every possible question. That would mean mastering the relevant material from sources as diverse as the Jewish and Christian Scriptures, the theological and liturgical traditions of the Christian East and West, the official teachings of the Church, and the contemporary social sciences. Any theologian who would attempt to do that would have to be equally expert at least in the methods of biblical criticism and historical and systematic theology as well as in a variety of disciplines such as sociology, anthropology, and comparative religions. Obviously Rahner does not take all these sources and disciplines into consideration, and in that sense his theology of worship is incomplete. But it was never his intention to answer any and every scholarly question. His goal is to provide a comprehensive explanation of worship that makes the Church's liturgy intelligible and credible for modern believers.

Rahner's main concern in developing a theology of worship is to interpret the Church's liturgy for people who are tempted to dismiss it as irrelevant, archaic, and superstitious. In particular, he wants to help those who believe that the experience of God, if it is to be found at all, will be found in the joys and struggles of "real" life and not in religious ritual. Rahner wants to provide these struggling believers with a comprehensive justification of worship that highlights the relationship between worship and the experience of God in ordinary life. In this way he hopes to show them that they can worship with intellectual integrity and honesty.[7]

The audience that Rahner envisions for his idea of worship determines the method with which he develops it. While he presumes that his readers are educated people who are able to wrestle with difficult ideas, he knows that they are not professional theologians. Even if he were able to delve into every facet of the theology of worship that might interest professionals, it would not be possible or appropriate to do so with this audience. Yet they require a clear and credible defense of worship that will speak to their questions and concerns. Rahner, then, provides a justification for the Church's liturgy on a level of discourse ap-

7. Ibid., 148–149.

propriate for this particular audience: a fundamental yet rigorous interpretation of the idea of worship for troubled believers, rather than a scholarly treatment of all the questions that might be raised by theologians.

Rahner does this by showing that acts of worship should not be seen as isolated interventions of grace into our otherwise profane and graceless lives, but as the symbolic expressions of what he calls "the liturgy of the world." The Church's liturgy is the symbolic manifestation of God's continual self-communication to us and our free response to God, a process which takes place throughout our lives and our history and which reached its highpoint and fulfillment in the death and resurrection of Christ. Rahner agrees with his audience that the experience of God is primarily to be found hidden in the midst of ordinary life, in our experiences of hope, responsibility, love, and death. We gather together in worship not because our lives are devoid of grace but because we need to express all the grace-filled moments of our lives, which are so easily overlooked or ignored.

Rahner's theology of worship, then, is firmly rooted in his theology of grace. In fact, he claims that it would be possible to deduce from his theology of grace "an entire theology of worship in all its aspects."[8] Liturgy is conventionally viewed as the means through which grace is made available to a world that is normally deprived of it. Rahner suggests, however, that what is celebrated in worship "is not something that does not occur or has not permanently occurred elsewhere in the world, but something that occurs always and everywhere . . . and is explicitly celebrated, stated and appropriated."[9] That "something," which is explicitly celebrated in worship, is the innermost, ever-present endowment of the world with the absolute mystery of God. The world is always and everywhere permeated with God's gracious self-communication. Salvation takes place whenever and wherever we freely accept this universal and continual engracing of the world. We express our free response to God's self-communication in the activities of our daily lives and not merely

8. Ibid., 145.
9. Ibid., 147.

when we participate in liturgy or other explicitly religious events, and so salvation can and does occur in the midst of our everyday lives. The ordinary and seemingly profane history of the world is the stage upon which takes place the continual drama of the self-communication of God and our acceptance of it. This is what Rahner means by "the liturgy of the world," namely, that "the world and its history are the terrible and sublime liturgy . . . which God celebrates and causes to be celebrated in and through human history in its freedom."[10] The Church's liturgy is the ritual celebration of this universal process of God's self-communication to the world and our free acceptance of God's self-gift. Worship, therefore, is to be seen "not as divine liturgy *in* the world, but as the divine liturgy *of* the world, as manifestation of the divine liturgy which is identical with salvation history."[11] For Rahner, the liturgy of the Church is the symbolic expression of the liturgy of the world.

Those who might expect Rahner to provide a complete systematic theology of worship will be disappointed; such was never his intention. It would be unfair to require him to answer all our scholarly questions, valid though they may be, since he never claimed that he could. But we can legitimately ask whether Rahner's idea of worship is an adequate response to the question he set out to address: How is worship related to the experience of God in everyday life? That continues to be an urgent question, and so Rahner's answer and its adequacy are of the greatest interest.

10. K. Rahner, "Considerations on the Active Role of the Person in the Sacramental Event," 169.
11. K. Rahner, "On the Theology of Worship," 149.

Chapter One

The Human Person as Spirit-in-the-World

The act of worship presupposes the extraordinary idea that we finite creatures are able to enter into a relationship with the infinite Creator. After all, Christians claim that in the liturgy we are graciously addressed by and gratefully respond to the absolute mystery of God. Worship is regularly described as a dialogue with God, an interpersonal self-communication in which God shares our lives and we participate in the life of God. Any basic defense of the idea of worship, therefore, must begin by establishing the possibility of such an experience of God. To do that, it must first show that we human beings are in fact open to an encounter with God. It is not at all apparent that any experience of an absolutely transcendent God is possible for beings who are as materially and historically conditioned as we obviously are. If we are so thoroughly a part of our world, is it possible for us to be open to something absolutely beyond our world without our ceasing to be human? Is it possible for us to know the unknowable, incomprehensible mystery which is God? In other words, is authentically *human* experience of God possible?

Secondly, if we are able to answer questions such as these affirmatively, a basic theology of worship would then have to explore the idea that God does in fact freely enter into our world and our lives without ceasing to be God. It is one thing to say that we are open to the possibility of experiencing God; it is quite another to explain what it means for the absolutely transcendent God to become really present to us and still remain transcendent. How is the absolute mystery present to us without being reduced to something finite and comprehensible? Is it reasonable to claim that in an experience of God we do not simply receive gifts *from* God, for example, enlightenment or empowerment, but the gift *of* God, real participation in God as

God? And is God authentically communicated to us as God only in the experience of worship? Finally, if we as human beings are in fact open to God and if God is in fact communicated to us as God, what would such a human experience of God be like? How, when, and where would such experiences take place? If the idea of worship as an authentic experience of God is to be justified, questions such as these must be addressed.

The first three chapters will explore these issues. This chapter will begin with Rahner's theological anthropology and the question of our openness to a relationship with God.[1] Rahner claims that the fundamental orientation to God which is presupposed by worship is in fact the essence of what it means to be human. Our openness to the absolute mystery of God is precisely what makes knowledge and freedom possible for us. Reflection on

1. The primary sources for the following are Karl Rahner, *Hearers of the Word*, trans. J. Donceel (Milwaukee: Marquette University Press, 1982); "Theology and Anthropology," TI 9 (New York: Seabury, 1977) 28–45; "The Theological Dimension of the Question About Man," TI 17 (New York: Crossroad, 1981) 53–70; *Hominisation: The Evolutionary Origin of Man as a Theological Problem* (Freiburg: Herder, 1965); "What Is Man?" *Christian at the Crossroads* (New York: Seabury, 1975) 11–20; and "Person": 2, "Man," C, "Theological," *Encyclopedia of Theology: The Concise Sacramentum Mundi* (New York: Crossroad, 1982) 1219–1225. The most significant secondary literature on Rahner's theological anthropology includes Peter Eicher, *Die anthropologische Wende: K. Rahners philosophischer Weg vom Wesen des Menschen zur personalen Existenz* (Freiburg, Schweiz: Universitätsverlag, 1970); Klaus P. Fischer, *Der Mensch als Geheimnis: Die Anthropologie Karl Rahners* (Freiburg: Herder, 1974); Gerald A. McCool, "Person and Community in Karl Rahner," *Person and Community*, ed. R. J. Roth (New York: Fordham University Press, 1975) 63–86; "The Philosophy of the Human Person in Karl Rahner's Theology," TS 22 (1961) 537–562; Josef Speck, *Karl Rahners theologische Anthropologie: Ein Einführung* (München: Kösel, 1967); Andrew Tallon, *Personal Becoming: Karl Rahner's Christian Anthropology* (Milwaukee: Marquette University Press, 1982); may also be found in *Thomist* 43 (1979) 7–177; "Rahner and Personization," *Philosophy Today* 14 (1970) 44–56; George Vass, *A Theologian in Search of a Philosophy: Understanding Karl Rahner*, Vol. I (London, England: Sheed and Ward, 1985); *The Mystery of Man and the Foundations of a Theological System: Understanding Karl Rahner*, Vol. II (London: Sheed and Ward, 1985); and Herbert Vorgrimler, "Der Begriff der Selbsttranszendenz in der Theologie Karl Rahners," *Wagnis Theologie: Erfahrungen mit der Theologie Karl Rahners*, hrsg. H. Vorgrimler (Freiburg: Herder, 1979) 242–258.

these basic human activities shows that we are fundamentally and inescapably oriented toward God. We are in the world and of the world, but we are simultaneously open to that which lies completely beyond the world. We are that part of the world which transcends the world. In Rahner's words, we are "spirit-in-the-world." We are in the world as beings who go beyond the world. Every fully human experience presupposes this openness to a relationship with God.

KNOWLEDGE AS AN EXPERIENCE OF TRANSCENDENCE

Early in his academic life, Rahner became convinced that a fundamental openness to the infinite mystery of God is the necessary condition that makes our knowledge of anything finite possible. This is the point at issue in his monumental study of Thomistic epistemology, *Spirit in the World*.[2] There Rahner interprets a particular Thomistic text[3] which raises the problem of how we can know anything beyond the world which we know through our senses. Or more specifically, how can we know the pure act of being, since it is not one of the beings of the material world which we know through our senses? The difficulty here is that Rahner, with Thomas, holds that we have no objective knowledge of any realities other than those that are present to us in the material, sensible world. As finite spirits we are dependent on sense intuition[4] for all our objective knowledge. But the pure act of being is not a finite, sensible being of our material world, and so it cannot be grasped in objective, conceptual knowledge. How then is it possible to know it? In other words, how are we historical beings able to know the transcendent God?

Rahner answers that while we are *finite* spirits and so are dependent upon sense intuition for our objective knowledge, we are nonetheless *spirits* capable of self-transcendence. We are only able to know objective realities because as spirits we transcend

2. Karl Rahner, *Spirit in the World* (Montreal: Palm Publishers, 1968). *See also* P. Eicher, *Die anthropologische Wende*, 72–78, 188–199, 233–256; and K. Fischer, *Der Mensch als Geheimnis*, 106–149.

3. *Summa theologiae* I, q. 84, a. 7.

4. This is what Thomas calls the *conversio ad phantasma*.

all objects of the material, temporal world and are open to the infinite horizon of absolute being.[5] In order to know anything as one thing and not something else, we must transcend it and grasp it against a horizon of other possibilities. We always comprehend the specific objects of our knowledge against some such horizon. Ultimately, we grasp any of these particular horizons against an unlimited horizon, which is beyond the realm of everything finite. This ultimate horizon cannot be an object of the same kind as the ones whose knowledge it makes possible. For then it, too, would be an object within our world and would require a horizon against which it could be known. The ultimate horizon must be that which cannot be transcended. The absolute horizon cannot be a particular being among other finite beings. Rather, it must be the ground of all being, infinite being.

A capacity to transcend particular beings and to be open to the limitless horizon, therefore, is the necessary condition of the possibility of our knowledge of anything in our finite world. It would be impossible for us to have any objective, conceptual knowledge of the finite realities of our world unless we were able to transcend those realities. If we really do know concrete, temporal, material objects in our world, we must have the capacity to transcend them. Such transcendence would mean that we are open to an ultimate horizon which lies beyond everything finite. Obviously, that horizon would be different from anything finite, material, or historical. And our knowledge or experience of that ultimate horizon would be different from our knowledge or experience of anything else. But the necessary condition which makes our knowledge of the objects of our world possible is this unique "knowledge" of a unique "object" which transcends our world. We do in fact know things in our world, and so it must be that we have this prior knowledge of the horizon of our world. The fact that we do know particular realities of our finite world shows that we are able to transcend them all. We may not

5. K. Rahner, *Spirit in the World*, 57.-383; *Hearers of the Word*, 48–58; and *Foundations of Christian Faith: An Introduction to the Idea of Christianity* (New York: Seabury, 1978) 14–23, 26–35.

be aware of this experience of transcendence; it may even be impossible for us to be directly, consciously, and conceptually aware of it, but such an experience is necessarily presupposed by the ordinary, conceptual knowledge we do have. Even the denial of such an experience of transcendence necessarily presupposes its reality. The act of saying that we know that we do not transcend ourselves would be an act of transcendence and so would affirm that which it is trying to deny.

We implicitly know, therefore, the infinite horizon of our world in the act of knowing any and every sensible, finite reality. Rahner uses the term *Vorgriff* (preapprehension, anticipation) to name this act of reaching out toward the unlimited horizon. We can only grasp specific finite objects by reaching out for the horizon of our world. Whenever we know any finite object, we do not grasp it merely by itself but simultaneously in relation to the ultimate horizon. This preapprehension does not occur before conceptual knowledge but, rather, is a constitutive element of such knowledge. The act of transcendence is not temporally but logically prior to our conceptual knowledge. At the same time that we know anything, we must always reach beyond it in a preapprehension of that which is beyond the realm of categorical realities. It is this ability to "know" infinite being that makes our knowledge of finite being possible. We are not normally aware of our preapprehension of the horizon of absolute being, and we can only conceptualize it with great difficulty. Nonetheless, it is an inescapable element of all our fully human activities.

We transcend anything that we know, reaching out beyond it for the horizon of absolute being. This horizon is not like any object we can know or conceptualize. Since we can only approach it as the infinite horizon of possibility simultaneously given with each finite object, it is not something we can master or control. It is the only thing we know that cannot be transcended, that has no horizon, and so it is clearly not a "thing" at all. It is the horizon for everything, not everything *else*, but for everything. Everything finite is finite because it has a horizon, because there is more beyond it. The ultimate horizon of all finite beings is infinite precisely because there is nothing more beyond it. This is what we point to with the word "God": the horizon which has no horizon. We reach out toward God without ever being able to transcend God.

Since this orientation to the God who transcends our world is the condition that makes any act of knowing possible, we implicitly "know" God every time we know any particular reality in our world. The preapprehension of God is the necessary condition for every act of human knowledge. Whenever we know anything, we always affirm the existence of God even though we do not conceptually and objectively grasp God. Every act of knowledge is an act of transcendence, and in every act of transcendence God is present and experienced as the goal of our transcendence. We implicitly know God as the goal of our transcendence whenever we know anything.

But we must be careful: The word "know" is being used equivocally here. The infinite horizon is different from anything finite, and so our knowledge of the horizon is different from our knowledge of the finite. Our knowledge of finite things is easily and directly conceptualized. Since we can go beyond finite things, we can comprehend them. We are in principle capable of seeing all the different sides of anything finite because we are able to transcend it. But we cannot transcend the ultimate horizon. We will never be able to go beyond or around God and see all the different sides of God. What we mean by "God" is precisely that which no one can go beyond. There is nothing beyond God to which we could go. There is no greater reality beyond God within which God could be completely categorized or adequately conceptualized.

The absolute mystery of God, therefore, can be known but never comprehended. We do have real knowledge of God, but it is not a knowledge that contains or captures God. God cannot be grasped conceptually the way the finite objects of our knowledge are grasped. The transcendental orientation of our spirits does not permit us to know the absolute being of God with the clarity of our conceptual knowledge of sensible objects. Rather, we know God as the absolute and unlimited horizon of our transcendence in the act of knowing the concrete, objective realties of our world. Our conceptual knowledge of historical realities always involves this implicit, nonconceptual awareness of the horizon of absolute mystery. (The opposite is also true: Our awareness of the absolute mystery of God is mediated by the concrete, historical objects of our conceptual knowledge.)

We overlook our implicit, nonconceptual knowledge of God precisely because it is a type of knowledge that is fundamentally different from our knowledge of anything finite. The only kind of knowledge that we are directly conscious of is our knowledge of finite things. This implicit knowledge of God is as impossible to conceptualize as God is. We cannot completely conceptualize or comprehend God because we cannot transcend God. Nor can we transcend the act of transcending ourselves. We cannot stand completely outside ourselves and know ourselves in the act of transcending. Whenever we attempt to transcend our act of transcending, we are always the ones attempting to transcend ourselves, and so we are unable to do so. We cannot both leave ourselves behind and watch ourselves leave ourselves behind. This is why it is so difficult to adequately conceptualize the way in which we know God. It is in fact impossible to do so: All we can do is to point in that direction.

Every conscious and fully human experience of our daily lives, therefore, involves an implicit knowledge of God. Although we normally overlook it, or even suppress it, we are always having to do with God even when we are caught up with the routine cares and concerns that fill our days. Experience of God is an inescapable, secret ingredient of our lives. Even when we turn all our attention to our knowledge of God, as we are doing now, we can never succeed in pinning it down. It always slips away from us; it is always just beyond our grasp. Nonetheless, such knowledge of God is a fact of everyday life even when we are conscious of everything else except God, even if we reject the very concept of God.

This transcendental orientation to God fundamentally determines who we are as human beings. Our openness to God is the ultimate, essential structure of who we are despite the fact that we are normally unaware of it. Transcendence is the very essence of human being:

"Man is spirit, i.e., he lives his life while reaching increasingly for the absolute, in openness towards God. And this openness towards God is not something which may happen or not happen to him once in a while, as he pleases. It is the condition of the possibility of that which is and has to be and always also is in his most humdrum daily life. Only that makes him into a man: that he is always already on the way to God, whether or not he knows it expressly, whether or not he wills it. He is forever the infinite openness of the finite for God."[6]

We are beings of absolute and unlimited transcendence, "always already on the way to God." Even though this transcendental orientation is a secret ingredient of daily life, it is unavoidable; it is present whether we are aware of it or not. This openness to the absolute mystery of God fundamentally and inescapably determines who we are. It can be overlooked, suppressed, or ignored, but it is always present as the condition that makes all human life possible. We are, therefore, that part of the finite world which is always open to the infinite. We are always part of the finite world, but at the same time we are always reaching beyond the finite world. We are both that part of the material world which has become spirit, and that part of spirit which has become material world.

FREEDOM AS AN EXPERIENCE OF TRANSCENDENCE

We have seen that our experience of knowing anything is always an experience of transcendence. Knowledge of finite things is possible for us because in every act of knowledge we reach beyond the things we know in a preapprehension of God. The same holds true for our freedom: It is also always an experience of transcendence. Every choice that we make is simultaneously a choice about some finite object as well as a choice made possible by and directed toward God. We are able to choose finite, limited goods because in willing them we simultaneously reach beyond them toward the unlimited horizon of God. This is not something that is at all readily apparent to us. To start with, we experience our historical and material conditioning much more graphically and insistently than we experience any ability to tran-

---

6. K. Rahner, *Hearers of the Word*, 57. *See also* "What Is Man?" 11-20.

scend such limitations. Such experiences lead many to conclude that we are completely determined by biological, sociological, and historical factors, and that freedom is only an illusion. Even if we acknowledge that we do have and make real choices, we normally experience those choices as finite. We see both the number of choices available in any particular situation and, more importantly, the objects and consequences of such choices, as finite. To the extent that we might think of God as an object of choice, we usually perceive any choices for or against God as being of exactly the same character as our choices about anything else. We make a number of choices about a number of things, and some of those choices may happen to be about God. God is seen as an object of freedom just like any finite object, and so decisions about God are seen as being no different than other decisions. The consequences of all such choices are seen as finite; freedom is seen primarily as freedom of choice, the ability to continually change and revise.[7]

The array of conflicting opinions about freedom indicates just how difficult it is to adequately conceptualize this basic human experience. But if freedom really is an experience of transcendence, it will in fact always be impossible to completely capture it. We transcend ourselves in every free act, but it is always we who are doing the transcending, and so we can never stand outside ourselves and catch ourselves in the act of such transcendence. There is a permanent and insurmountable difference between our basic experiences of freedom and our theories about those experiences. There is always more happening in the experience of freedom than we can be explicitly and directly aware

7. The principal sources for Rahner's theology of freedom are Karl Rahner, ''Theology of Freedom,'' TI 6 (New York: Crossroad, 1982) 178–196; ''The Dignity and Freedom of Man,'' TI 2 (Baltimore: Helicon, 1963) 246–263; ''Freedom in the Church,'' TI 2 (Baltimore: Helicon, 1963) 89–107; Foundations of Christian Faith, 35–39: ''On the Theology of Freedom,'' Freedom and Man, ed. J. C. Murray (New York: Kenedy, 1965) 201–217; Grace in Freedom (New York: Herder and Herder, 1969) 203–261; and ''Freedom'': 2, ''Theological,'' Encyclopedia of Theology: The Concise Sacramentum Mundi, 544–545. See also Robert L. Hurd, ''The Concept of Freedom in Rahner,'' Listening 17 (1982) 138–152.

of. The transcendental dimension of freedom, like the transcendental dimension of knowledge, always lies just beyond our conceptual grasp. The best we can do is to point in that direction, convinced that such transcendence is the necessary condition of the possibility of our free acts. We know that every act of freedom must be an experience of transcendence because any attempt to deny that would affirm it. The denial of freedom would be a free act and would necessarily affirm that which it was denying.

We can only choose particular, finite goods if we are able to transcend them and grasp them against the horizon of absolute good. Whenever we make a choice, we select something against a background of various goods. We always choose specific goods against some such horizon of good things. Ultimately, we grasp these particular horizons against an unlimited horizon which is beyond the realm of all particular goods. The ultimate horizon cannot be a finite good, or a set of finite goods, of the same kind as the ones for which it provides the horizon, for then it too would require some more-ultimate horizon of good beyond it in order for it to be good. Openness to a horizon of absolute good, therefore, is the necessary condition of the possibility of choosing any finite good. If we do in fact make real choices about finite goods, then we must be open to the ultimate horizon of good. The ultimate horizon of good is different from any particular good, and so the relationship of our freedom to this horizon is different from the relationship of our freedom to any finite good.

An implicit element of every free act, then, is our transcendental openness to God. Our freedom is made possible by the fact that we are able to reach out to God. Theologically speaking, freedom should not be understood simply as freedom of choice, a neutral capacity which arbitrarily selects between various objects. Freedom is more than mere freedom of choice because whenever freedom is exercised and no matter what its object is, it is always also involved with God. Every experience of freedom involves a basic, implicit experience of our orientation to God. A free act is always an event in which we are reaching beyond ourselves and beyond limited goods toward the unlimited goodness of God. We are normally unaware of this dimension of our choices, and it is in fact impossible for us to directly observe it or completely comprehend it. But it is, nonetheless, a secret ingredient of every choice we make no matter how mundane that choice might be. The exercise of our freedom is always an anonymous experience of our orientation to God.

God, therefore, should not be thought of as one among many possible objects of the freedom of choice. God is present in every free act as its supporting ground and ultimate orientation. By being the unlimited horizon of good, God makes our freedom possible. We could not make particular choices unless we could transcend ourselves and open ourselves toward the ultimate horizon. And we could not transcend ourselves unless there were an ultimate horizon toward which we could reach. We do not make our transcendence possible, God makes it possible by being the ultimate goal which draws our transcendence forth. God is the original source of our freedom and is present in every decision we make as its supporting ground. God can never be just another object about which we make choices.

Freedom is not only made possible by God; it is also freedom in relation to God. This is the most startling assertion of the Christian understanding of freedom. If God is understood merely as one of the many objects of a neutral, independent freedom of choice, the idea that freedom is freedom even in relation to God would present no particular difficulty. But God is not just another object of freedom, God is the ground of the possibility of our freedom and its ultimate goal. Every time we make a choice about some particular good, we make that choice against the absolute horizon of good. In every choice we not only affirm some particular good, we also affirm or deny the ultimate horizon of good. Whenever we freely take a stand about anything, we take a stand for or against God. Every act of freedom, no matter how ordinary and seemingly inconsequential it might be, is always also a choice about God.

We should note here that our transcendence is not simply a natural dynamism directed toward God as the distant horizon. In the world in which we do in fact live, our transcendence is never simply given to us as something "natural." It is always embraced and taken up by the self-communication of God. God is not present to us merely as the asymptotic horizon of our transcendence, a goal we eternally approach but never reach. In grace, God is actually communicated to us. Ultimately, this is the reason why our freedom toward the ground of our transcendence is given an immediacy to God by which it becomes radically capable of saying yes or no to God. So even though freedom is always exercised in relation to the concrete individual things of experience, it is unavoidably concerned with God. Freedom is fundamentally the freedom of taking a stand toward God.

In the Christian view, then, we have the freedom to deny the God upon whom we are completely dependent for our freedom. The paradox of this is that we are able to culpably deny God, the source of our freedom, in an act that would simultaneously and necessarily reaffirm the dependence of our freedom upon God. This does not mean that we are in a position of neutrality in relation to God, or that denial of God is the same kind of act as the affirmation of God. The no by which we deny God, since it simultaneously reaffirms our dependence on God, is an inherently absurd act. It is, therefore, qualitatively different from the yes by which we affirm our dependence on God. Nor does it mean that in every concrete act of freedom we are making our fundamental choice for or against God all over again. While all choices involve our orientation to God, they do not all engage that freedom to the same degree. Some choices touch our relationship to God in only peripheral ways. Our choices about one another involve a much more immediate affirmation or denial of God because these objects of our freedom are also subjects who are essentially oriented to God. This explains the unity of the love of neighbor and the love of God.

But our freedom does include the possibility of a culpable and contradictory denial of its source. This indicates just how radically free we really are. We know that we are not completely free: We experience our freedom as conditioned by a wide variety of limitations. That is all part of the fact that we are radically historical and material beings. But the very fact that we experience our freedom as limited means that we experience ourselves as going beyond those limits in some way. We would not know ourselves as limited unless we also transcended ourselves.

We cannot, then, be completely determined by our historical and material conditions. Our ability to transcend ourselves enables us to make free choices. Whenever we do make such choices, at some level we simultaneously make a choice about the ultimate ground of our existence. We are so radically free that we are actually able to affirm or deny God. This is the paradox of being human: that we are radically conditioned and radically free at the same time. We experience our historicity through our transcendence, and our transcendence through our historicity. This is but one dimension of the more basic paradox of human existence, that is, that we are spirit-in-the-world.

The basic free choice that we make for or against God is also a basic choice about ourselves. We are so radically free that we actually become the choice we make toward God. By making choices that affirm God, we ourselves become an affirmation of God; by making choices that deny God, we ourselves become a denial of God. Choices about God are always choices about ourselves. Freedom, then, is not only freedom toward God. It is also necessarily our freedom in relation to ourselves, the capacity to make ourselves once and for all. We do not merely perform actions that always pass away again; we become our freedom. By our free decisions we really become so good or evil in the very ground of our being itself that our final salvation or damnation is already given in this, even though it is hidden. Freedom is the capacity for a definitive self-realization.

By becoming an affirmation or a denial of God, then, we become an affirmation or denial of ourselves. The affirmation of God is always an affirmation of that essential openness to God which is our most distinctive characteristic as human beings. Conversely, the denial of God is a futile and absurd attempt to deny that basic orientation of our being which makes it possible for us to deny God. It is not only a rebellion against God, it is also a rebellion against ourselves. When we fundamentally deny God, we become our own self-denial. When we fundamentally affirm God, we become our own self-affirmation.

This also means that choices about ourselves are essentially choices about God. We have already seen that every choice about any particular object of our freedom involves at some level a choice about the source and ultimate horizon of our freedom. Our free responses to one another involve an especially profound response to God because these objects of our freedom are also subjects who are essentially related to God. We cannot separate another person from that person's relationship to God, because that person *is* a relationship to God. Our self-choices are also choices about subjects who are essentially oriented toward God. And in our choices about ourselves, we can be even more immediately present to someone who is oriented toward God than we can be in our choices about one another. Our most basic choices for or against God are often made in the process of making our basic choices to affirm or deny ourselves. The love of God and the love of neighbor are inseparably connected to the love of self.

Freedom, therefore, is not merely the quality of an act or a capacity exercised at some time. Freedom is an essential characteristic of human existence itself. Freedom is the possibility of saying yes or no to ourselves. It is never simply the choice between individual objects but is always our *self*-exercise. We are basic objects of our own freedom, and all specific objects in the world around us are objects of freedom only insofar as they mediate ourselves to ourselves. Freedom essentially involves the power to decide about ourselves and to actualize ourselves. This finalizing self-realization is a characteristic of freedom that is most clearly evident in death. Until death, all our decisions are always open to change and revision, and our freedom is never able to integrate completely all the dimensions of our lives. But death is the event in which we actively sum up our lives, and so it is the event in which we make an irreversible decision about ourselves.[8]

Our free self-realization before God is always mediated by the categorical realities of time and space, of our materiality and our

8. For Rahner's theology of death *see* Karl Rahner, *On the Theology of Death* (Montreal: Palm Publishers, 1961); "On Christian Dying," TI 7 (New York: Seabury, 1977) 285–293; "Theological Considerations on the Moment of Death," TI 11 (New York: Crossroad, 1982) 309–321; "Ideas for a Theology of Death," TI 13 (New York: Crossroad, 1983) 169–186; and "Christian Dying," TI 18 (New York: Crossroad, 1983) 226–256.

history. This points to the way in which the transcendental and the categorical mutually condition one another in Rahner's theology. He says, "It has always been clear in my theology that a 'transcendental experience' (of God and of grace) is always mediated through a categorical experience in history, in interpersonal relationships, and in society."[9] Thus, for Rahner, our transcendental knowledge of God as horizon is not a direct, conceptual grasp of God but rather a nonconceptual awareness mediated by the knowledge of concrete, historical realities.

Likewise, our transcendental freedom in relation to God and ourselves is necessarily expressed and exercised in relation to the concrete and objective realties of life. Rahner acknowledges that the freedom by which we realize ourselves can be expressed in explicitly religious events like worship. "Yet, precisely this freedom of the corporeal, social and historical creature which is man is always and necessarily a freedom which is exercised through an encounter with the world—the community and environment in which man lives; its nature combines both that of transcendental freedom and of a particular category of freedom."[10] The exercise of freedom shows that we are transcendent beings precisely as historical beings and historical beings precisely as transcendent beings. Our subjective essence of unlimited transcendentality is mediated to us historically in our free self-realization. Therefore, history is ultimately the history of freedom and transcendentality. Transcendence always has a history, and history is always the event of this transcendence.

Examination of the basic human activities of knowing and choosing reveals, then, that a transcendental openness to the absolute mystery of God is the essence of being human. It is precisely because we are able to transcend ourselves that we know anything, that we are free and responsible, and, therefore, that we are persons and subjects. This transcendence is what makes us human: We are radically historical and radically transcendent.

9. Karl Rahner, "Introduction," in James J. Bacik, *Apologetics and the Eclipse of Mystery: Mystagogy According to Karl Rahner* (Notre Dame: University of Notre Dame Press, 1980) x.
10. Karl Rahner, "History of the World and Salvation-History," TI 5 (New York: Crossroad, 1983) 98.

We are spirit-in-the-world. To be human is to be a concrete, material, embodied being fundamentally open to the unfathomable mystery. Our transcendental orientation can be suppressed or ignored, but it is always present as the condition that makes our subjectivity possible. This transcendental orientation is not something we create; it is not a matter of our own minds creating the space within which we know or choose things. The goal of our transcendence is also its source. Our knowledge of God is made possible by God, and so the transcendence which makes us human is in that sense already an experience of grace.

Thus we do have the potential for the sort of dialogical relationship with God which is presupposed in worship. In fact, we implicitly know and respond to the absolute mystery of God in all our daily activities. Our experience of ordinary daily life presupposes a relationship with God, and our relationship with the absolutely transcendent God is mediated by ordinary daily human life. This has enormously important implications for our understanding of worship. It means that when we direct ourselves to the explicit worship of God, we are not entering into a relationship with God as though none had existed previously. On the contrary, when we worship, our relationship with that unfathomable mystery, which is a secret ingredient of every moment of our daily lives, is accepted and expressed. Furthermore, it should not be surprising that our relationship with the transcendent God in worship is mediated by the particular and the historical: by material objects such as water, oil, bread and wine, by word and song, by symbol and ritual. Our experience of anything historical is always also an experience of God, and our experience of God is always mediated by the historical. We are transcendent beings precisely as historical beings, a fact which receives special expression in worship.

THE HUMAN PERSON AS EMBODIED SPIRIT: REAL SYMBOLS

Rahner's notion of the real symbol is rooted in his theological anthropology.[11] For Rahner, a real symbol is distinct from the re-

11. For Rahner's theology of real symbols *see* Karl Rahner, "The Theology of the Symbol," TI 4 (Baltimore: Helicon, 1966) 221–252. *See also* James J.

ality that is symbolized, but is so derived from and so united with that reality that the reality symbolized is really made present. A real symbol is both a symbol, and therefore distinct from the reality it symbolizes, and the real presence of the reality it symbolizes. In a real symbol, both a symbol and a reality distinct from the symbol are given together and inseparably. The real symbol and the reality symbolized are both identified and not identified with each other. The best example we have of a real symbol is the human body. And the best way of understanding the relationship between our body and our soul, between our historical, material dimension and our transcendental, spiritual dimension, is the notion of the real symbol. This notion will play an integral part in Rahner's theology of worship, so we will explore it briefly.

Using the Thomistic view of the human person, Rahner sees the body as the symbol of the soul because the body is formed as the self-realization of the soul, even though inadequately. Nonetheless, the soul renders itself present in the body, which is distinct from it. The body is derived from the soul, and, therefore, it corresponds to the soul. This makes it possible for the body to be the way in which the soul is present to itself and to others. The body, therefore, is the real symbol of the soul.

In other words, the body is the real symbol of the self. We know that there is a real distinction in the human person between the body and the self. We cannot be reduced to the body; we are something more. The body is not simply identical with the self. One can, for example, give one's body to another person without giving one's self. The body can go through dramatic and fundamental changes without the self changing. We believe that the body will die without the self ceasing to exist. But at the same time, we recognize that the body is united to and somehow derived from the self. The body is more than a possession; it so completely comes from the self and expresses the self that it is

Buckley, "On Being a Symbol: An Appraisal of Karl Rahner," TS 40 (1979) 453–473; and C. Annice Callahan, "Karl Rahner's Theology of Symbol: Basis for His Theology of the Church and the Sacraments," Irish Theological Quarterly 49 (1982) 195–205.

the way in which we are present to the self and to others. We could not be ourselves or be present to one another without being embodied. Every way in which we do manage to give ourselves to one another is somehow bodily. The body, then, is the real symbol of the self: It is distinct from what it symbolizes but so expresses what it symbolizes that the reality symbolized is made really present.

This relationship between the body and the self is the best example we have of the relationship between a real symbol and what it symbolizes. Real symbols must be distinguished from other modes of symbolic representation. Symbolic representations are only a secondary form of symbolic being, merely arbitrary signs, signals, and codes. Such signs occur when two realities, each of which is thought to be already self-contained and directly intelligible by itself, "agree" with one another in some fashion. This "agreement" is seen to make it possible for the better known and more accessible of the two to refer to the other and call attention to it, and hence to be used as a "symbol" for the other. Such symbolic representation is an inferior mode of symbolism. If this were the only kind of symbol, then symbols could only be distinguished from one another by the degree and precise mode of this secondary similarity between the two realities. In the long run that would mean that anything could be the symbol of anything else, since everything agrees with everything else in some way or another.

Admittedly, the margins between merely arbitrary signs and genuine symbols are fluid. But there is a way in which one reality can represent another, which is far less arbitrary than that involved in signs and signals. This deeper kind of representation is what is meant here by a real symbol: the supreme and primal form of representation in which one reality renders another reality present. But what are the philosophical and theological foundations for this concept of a real symbol?

The fact that every being is multiple is axiomatic in the ontology of finite being. Every finite being bears the stigma of being finite by the very fact that it is not absolutely simple. Only infinite being is absolutely simple. Finite being has of itself a real multiplicity (as essence and existence) within the permanent unity of its reality. This does not mean, however, that an intrinsic plurality must always be merely the stigma of the finiteness of a being. On the contrary, the mystery of the Trinity shows that there is a true and real, even though relative, distinction of persons in the supreme simplicity of God and to that extent a plurality. Therefore, it is quite possible that the pluralism of the finite creature is not merely a negative consequence and indication of its finiteness. It could also be a consequence, even though only recognizable through revelation as such, of that divine plurality which does not imply imperfection and limitation of being but the supreme fullness of unity. Therefore, being is plural in itself. A being is of itself plural in its unity.

Because of the unity of a being, however, the plural moments in a being must have an inner agreement among themselves. This unity cannot be the subsequent conjunction of separate elements that once stood on their own, because that would imply a denial of the unity of the being. The plurality must be in an original and an originally superior unity. Such unity can only exist if the plural moments are derived from an original unity.

Thus, each being as a unity possesses a plurality that is derived from an original unity. But whatever exists derivatively, and hence is united with its origin while still being distinct from it, must be considered as the expression of the origin and of the primordial unity. The agreement with its origin of that which is constituted as derivative within the unity is, in a certain sense, the constitution of the derivative as a symbol.

Since this is true for being in general, we may say that each being forms, in its own way, more or less perfectly according to its degree of being, something distinct from itself and yet one with itself for its own fulfillment. This differentiated being, which is originally one, is in agreement because derivative and, because derivatively in agreement, is expressive. The mystery of the Trinity shows that the "one" of unity and plurality thus understood is an ontological ultimate, a perfection of being. Being as such, and hence as one, for the fulfillment of its being and its unity, emerges into a plurality. The supreme mode of this is the Trinity.

Thus, every being possesses a plurality as an intrinsic element of its unity. This plurality constitutes itself because of its origin from an original unity as the way to fulfill the unity of the being (or in the case of the Trinity, on account of the unity already perfect) in such a way that that which is originated and different is in agreement with its origin and therefore has the character of an expression or "symbol" with regard to its origin. The first principle of Rahner's ontology of symbols, then, is that all beings are by their nature symbolic, because they necessarily express themselves in order to attain their own nature.

The self-constitutive act whereby a being constitutes itself as a plurality makes self-possession in knowledge and love possible. A being "comes to itself" in its expression. It comes to itself to the extent to which it realizes itself by constituting a plurality. Each being, inasmuch as it has and realizes being, is itself primarily "symbolic." It expresses itself and possesses itself by doing so. Therefore, a symbol is not to be primarily considered as a secondary relationship between two different beings in which one is seen to represent the other by an outside observer. A being is also "symbolic" in itself because the expression, which it retains while constituting it as the "other," is the way in which it communicates itself to itself in knowledge and love. In other words, the symbol is not originally for the benefit of others. The "symbol" is originally the way of knowledge of self and possession of self.

This is the way we can arrive at a theory of the symbol where the symbol is the reality in which another attains knowledge of a being. A being can be and is known insofar as it is originally symbolic in itself and for itself. Rahner says, therefore, that the primordial meaning of the symbol and the symbolic, according to which each being is in itself and for itself symbolic, and hence symbolic for another, is that

"as a being realizes itself in its own intrinsic 'otherness' (which is constitutive of its being), retentive of its intrinsic plurality (which is contained in its self-realization) as its derivative and hence congruous expression, it makes itself known. This derivative and congruous expression, constitutive of each being, is the symbol which comes in addition from the object of knowledge to the knower—in addition only because already initially present in the depths of the grounds of each one's being. The being is known in this symbol, without which it cannot be known at all; thus it is symbol in the original (transcendental) sense of the word."[12]

Or to put it more simply, the symbol is primarily the self-realization of a being in the other, which is constitutive of its essence.

Rahner thinks that the whole of theology is incomprehensible if it is not seen essentially as a theology of symbols. We have already seen that the Trinity figures into his theology of the symbol. Augustinian Trinitarian theology maintains that the Word is generated by the Father and is the image and expression of the Father. It sees this process as necessarily given with the divine act of self-knowledge. For Rahner, this means that the Word is the symbol of the Father, "the inward symbol which remains distinct from what is symbolized, which is constituted by what is symbolized, where what is symbolized expresses itself and possesses itself."[13] The incarnate Word is the absolute symbol of God in the world because he is filled as nothing else can be with God. The humanity of Christ is not an arbitrary sign that would be able only to represent God but not make God present. The humanity of Christ is the self-disclosure of the Word itself. It is what appears when God expresses himself. And so Christ in his humanity is the revelatory symbol in which God is rendered present in the world.

The Church, since it is the ongoing presence of Christ in the world, continues his symbolic function. Because the grace of salvation, the Holy Spirit, is of its essence, the Church is the primary symbol of the grace of God for the world. It is the full symbol of the eschatologically triumphant grace of Christ. The sacraments are real symbols that make the symbolic reality of the Church concrete. They both effect what they symbolize and symbolize what they effect. This they can do precisely because they are real symbols of the Church.

Rahner employs the notion of the real symbol in the widest variety of theological topics. God's salvific action always takes place

12. K. Rahner, "Theology of the Symbol," 231.
13. Ibid., 236.

in such a way that God is the reality of salvation. Salvation, therefore, is given to us and grasped by us through real symbols. These symbols are not arbitrary signs; they really exhibit and make present the reality that they symbolize: God. So it should not be surprising that the notion of the real symbol will play an important part in Rahner's theology of worship. All his writings on worship are directly or indirectly based on his philosophical and theological analysis of the character of the symbol.

Chapter Two

The Self-Communication of God

We have been defending the idea that worship is an experience
of interpersonal communion in which God shares our lives and
we participate in the life of God. In Chapter 1, we saw that it is
possible for us to enter into such a relationship with God. Even
though we human beings are radically conditioned by matter and
history, we are also inescapably oriented to that which completely transcends our world. We always experience our world in
and through our experience of the transcendent, and we always
experience the goal of our transcendence as the unsurpassable
horizon beyond something finite and categorical. We are spirit-in-
the-world, and so it is possible for us to be open to God without
ceasing to be human. This simultaneous orientation to the transcendent and the categorical is in fact what is most characteristically human about us. In every authentic and fully human
experience, no matter how ordinary and everyday it might seem,
we implicitly experience our openness to the infinite transcendent God.

Our idea of worship, however, presupposes that we do not
simply have an implicit experience of God as the inaccessible and
essentially incomprehensible goal of our transcendence; we also
have an explicit experience of God as the near and immediately
available fulfillment of our openness to the infinite. Worship is
not merely the offering of ourselves to God; it is also the receiving of grace and salvation from God. In worship, we experience
our orientation to God and, more importantly, God's orientation
to us. There is a dialogical quality to worship, and if we are to
understand how truly extraordinary this event is, we must look
not only at ourselves and what we are open to hearing from God
but at God and what God freely communicates to us. Christians
believe that God enters into communion with us without ceasing

to be God. God is not reduced in the process to something finite, manageable, and comprehensible, but always remains absolute mystery. What is communicated to us in worship, then, is not some gift *from* God, but the gift *of* God. This gift of God's gracious self-communication is not, however, only available in the experience of worship. It is always and everywhere present in the world and in human experience at least as an invitation.

GOD AS ABSOLUTE MYSTERY

We cannot explain how it is possible for God, without ceasing to be God, to freely enter into the kind of interpersonal communion with us that we suggest takes place in worship. In order to do so, we would need to comprehend the absolute incomprehensibility of God. Christians simply claim that they know God can do this because they know that God does do this. If God cannot be united with us as God, then we have not been saved, for what does salvation mean if not union with God? Christians believe that through God's gracious self-communication, we are invited to participate in God, and so to be transformed and become like God. The question is, what do we mean by this? What does it mean to say that the horizon of our transcendence comes near to us?

The ultimate horizon of our transcendence is present to us as that which is always indefinable and unattainable. The goal toward which our transcendence is oriented is that which makes it possible for us to categorize and conceptualize all the finite objects we know. Since it is the ultimate horizon of our transcendence, it cannot be brought within the horizon and distinguished from finite things. It is the supreme limit by which everything is defined, and so it cannot itself be defined by a still more ultimate limit. The infinite expanse which can and does encompass everything cannot itself be encompassed. It is that which is absolutely indefinable and incomprehensible. In other words, it is absolute mystery.[1]

1. For Rahner's theology of mystery and of God as absolute mystery, *see* Karl Rahner, "The Concept of Mystery in Catholic Theology," TI 4 (New York: Crossroad, 1982) 36–73; "An Investigation of the Incomprehensibility

We know this horizon of our transcendence only as that which makes our grasp of finite beings possible. It is present in our experiences of transcendence only as something distant and aloof; the asymptotic goal which is always just beyond our reach. But we are always in the presence of this absolute mystery even when we are dealing with the most ordinary and comprehensible realities of our finite world. We live by virtue of the absolute mystery whether we are explicitly conscious of it or not.

For Rahner, these experiences of the goal of our transcendence are our original experiences of the holy mystery of God.

"The nameless being which is at the disposal of none and disposes of all, which rules over transcendence by being loving freedom, is uniquely and precisely that which we can call 'holy' in the strict and original sense. For how should one name the nameless, sovereign beloved, which relegates us to our finitude, except as 'holy,' and what could we call holy if not this? Or to what does the name 'holy' belong more primordially than to the infinite Whither of receptive love which before this incomprehensible and inexpressible being becomes trembling adoration? In transcendence therefore is found, in the form of the aloof and distant which rules unruled, the nameless being which is infinitely holy. This we call mystery, or rather, the *holy mystery*."[2]

of God in St. Thomas Aquinas," TI 16 (New York: Crossroad, 1983) 244–254; "The Human Question of Meaning in Face of the Absolute Mystery of God," TI 18 (New York: Crossroad, 1983) 89–104; "The Hiddenness of God," TI 16 (New York: Crossroad, 1983) 227–243; "Mystery," *Encyclopedia of Theology: The Concise* Sacramentum Mundi (New York: Crossroad, 1982) 1000–1004; "Being Open to God as Ever Greater," TI 7 (New York: Seabury, 1977) 25–46; "The Experience of God Today," TI 11 (New York: Crossroad, 1982) 149–165; *Hearers of the Word* (Milwaukee: Marquette University Press, 1982) 59–79; and *Foundations of Christian Faith: An Introduction to the Idea of Christianity* (New York: Seabury, 1978) 44–89. *See also* James J. Bacik, *Apologetics and the Eclipse of Mystery: Mystagogy According to Karl Rahner* (Notre Dame: University of Notre Dame Press, 1980); and John J. Mawhinney, "The Concept of Mystery in Karl Rahner's Philosophical Theology," *Union Seminary Quarterly Review* 24 (1968) 17–30.

2. K. Rahner, "The Concept of Mystery in Catholic Theology," 53.

In other words, Rahner claims that the absolute mystery which we experience as the horizon of our transcendence is what we mean by "God."

Rahner ordinarily refers to God as the absolute, holy mystery. When he does so, however, he is not simply identifying God with the concept of absolute mystery. Such a move would assume that our concept of God includes some positive content, which could then be equated with the positive content in our concept of absolute mystery. Both the terms "God" and "absolute mystery" are affirmations of the eternal and essential ineffability of that which we experience as the horizon of our transcendence. Naming the absolute, holy mystery "God" does not describe God. On the contrary, it reminds us that none of our language about God ever really captures who God is. Rahner prefers to name the goal of our transcendence the "absolute, holy mystery" because the word "God" has become so familiar to us that we normally forget its apophatic character. We need to return over and over again to our experiences of absolute mystery to catch some glimmer of what is meant by "God."[3]

3. For Rahner's treatment of the doctrine of God, see Karl Rahner, "Observations on the Doctrine of God in Catholic Dogmatics," TI 9 (New York: Seabury, 1977) 127–144; "*Theos* in the New Testament," TI 1 (Baltimore: Helicon, 1961), 79–148; "God": 3, "Doctrine of God," *Encyclopedia of Theology: The Concise Sacramentum Mundi*, 568–572; *Grace in Freedom*, 183–202; *The Trinity* (New York: Seabury, 1974); "The Mystery of the Trinity," TI 16 (New York: Crossroad, 1983) 255–259; "Remarks on the Dogmatic Treatise 'De Trinitate,' " TI 4 (New York: Crossroad, 1982) 77–102; and "Oneness and Threefoldness of God in Discussion with Islam," TI 18 (New York: Crossroad, 1983) 105–121. *See also* Anne Carr, "The God Who Is Involved," *Theology Today* 38 (1981) 314–328; Joseph Donceel, "Second Thoughts on the Nature of God," *Thought* 46 (1971) 346–370; William J. Hoye, *Die Verfinsterung des Absoluten Geheimnisses: Eine Kritik der Gotteslehre Karl Rahners* (Düsseldorf: Patmos, 1979); J. Norman King, *The God of Forgiveness and Healing in the Theology of Karl Rahner* (Lanham, Md.: University Press of America, 1982); Piet Schoonenberg, "Zur Trinitätslehre Karl Rahners," *Glaube im Prozess: Christsein nach dem II. Vatikanum, Für Karl Rahner*, hrsg. E. Klinger + K. Wittstadt (Freiburg: Herder, 1984) 471–491; Eberhard Jüngel, "Das Verhältnis von "ökonomischer" und "immanenter" Trinität," *ZThK* 72 (1975) 353–364; Catherine M. LaCunga, "Re-Conceiving the Trinity as the Mystery of Salvation," *Scottish Journal of Theology* 38 (1985) 1–23; and Mark

The notion of mystery that Rahner is using here is not the conventional one, where it is presupposed that mystery is primarily a characteristic of a statement. Even though the objects referred to by statements are called mysteries, in the conventional notion it is the statements themselves that have the quality of mystery. We routinely assume that there are a number of these mysteries, all made up of truths considered to be only provisionally incomprehensible. That is to say, given the information currently available to us, we are not able to solve these mysteries, but there is no reason to assume that they are necessarily insolvable, or that at some time in the future they will not in fact be solved.

In the realm of religious matters, the "mysteries of the faith" are seen as affirmations whose truth can be guaranteed only by a divine communication. They do not become clear even when communicated by divine revelation but remain for now the objects of faith. They are distinguished from the truths of natural reason, which can be "seen," "comprehended," and "demonstrated." The conventional notion of mystery, therefore, is defined in relationship to human reason: A mystery is something we do not understand. Reason is interpreted as a faculty that is oriented to evidence, insight, and strict proof. It is assumed that the mysteries of the faith are obscure and impenetrable for now, but will be clarified in the beatific vision and so finally meet the demands made by human reason for insight and clarity.[4]

The conventional notion of mystery is inconsistent with the tradition that says that God remains incomprehensible even when seen "face to face." According to that tradition, the object of the beatific vision is precisely the divine incomprehensibility. The beatific vision means grasping and being grasped by the absolute mystery. This supreme act of knowledge is not the abolition or diminution of the mystery but its eternal and total immediacy. There is no reason to suppose that God becomes any less of a mystery in the beatific vision simply because we now experience God directly and immediately. If this beatific vision is our salva-

Lloyd Taylor, *God Is Love: A Study in the Theology of Karl Rahner* (Atlanta: Scholars' Press, 1986).
4. K. Rahner, "The Concept of Mystery in Catholic Theology," 37–41.

tion, and therefore the fulfillment of human knowing, our conventional understanding of reason must be revised. Reason can no longer be described as a faculty that is primarily and essentially ordered toward the mastery of clear and distinct ideas. Its greatest and highest act is the immediate knowledge of the absolute mystery. And if our understanding of reason is revised, our notion of mystery must also change. Mystery should not be seen as a limitation of knowledge that ought to be clear and distinct. It is the highest object of human reason.[5]

The conventional notion of mystery is also inconsistent with the transcendental character of the human spirit. Our spirits reach for the incomprehensible inasmuch as they press on beyond the actual finite objects of comprehension to an anticipatory "grasp" of the unreachable horizon. The goal of this anticipatory grasp, which the transcendence of our spirits knows without comprehending, is not a preliminary sphere of darkness that is gradually lit up. As the transcendental condition of the possibility of objective knowledge, it lies ever beyond the reach of such knowledge. Human reason, therefore, lives by the indefinable and the incomprehensible. Reason is the very faculty which is originally and basically a grasp of mystery, and, only derivatively, reason in the ordinary sense of the word.

In our experiences of transcendence, we meet God as the holy mystery. Since every human experience is an experience of transcendence, since in every experience we reach out toward the boundless horizon of absolute mystery, this mystery in all its incomprehensibility is self-evident in human life.

"If transcendence is not something which we practice on the side as a metaphysical luxury of our intellectual existence, but if this transcendence is rather the plainest, most obvious and most necessary condition of possibility for *all* spiritual understanding and comprehension, then the holy mystery really is the one

5. Karl Rahner, "Beatific Vision," *Encyclopedia of Theology: The Concise Sacramentum Mundi*, 78–80; "An Investigation of the Incomprehensibility of God in St. Thomas," 245–247; "The Hiddenness of God," 228–235; "The Human Question of Meaning in Face of the Absolute Mystery of God," 90–92.

thing that is self-evident, the one thing which is grounded in itself even from our point of view. For all other understanding, however clear it might appear, is grounded in this transcendence. All clear understanding is grounded in the darkness of God."[6]

As we shall see more deeply when we explore Rahner's theology of grace, the distant and aloof horizon of natural transcendence comes near and becomes accessible in and through God's self-communication. But even though grace brings us an immediate access to God, it does not in any way make God less of a mystery. Grace does not imply the elimination of the mystery but the radical possibility of the absolute proximity of the mystery. The absolute mystery is not reduced by its proximity, but is really presented as mystery. Grace and its fulfillment in the beatific vision are the possibility and the reality respectively of the immediate presence of the absolute, holy mystery. The experience of grace is the experience of the presence of the abiding mystery of God.

The "mysteries of the faith" are a secondary and derived phenomenon. There are only three truths that can be regarded as mysteries strictly speaking: the Trinity, the incarnation, and the divinization of the human person in grace and glory.[7] These three can be divided into two groups: the Trinitarian mystery of God in itself, and the mystery of the incarnation and grace, insofar as these last two deal with a relationship of God to the nondivine. The possibility that a finite, created reality could be endowed with the infinite, which is not imparted or represented by a finite gift and through the possession of which one "partakes" of God, constitutes the incomprehensibility of the incarnation and grace. Since the absolute mystery of God is communicated to us in the incarnation and grace, these two mysteries are simply radical forms of the primordial one: God as the holy and abiding mystery for the creature, not as something distant and remote but in radical proximity. Rahner says that all

6. K. Rahner, *Foundations of Christian Faith*, 21–22.
7. K. Rahner, "The Concept of Mystery in Catholic Theology," 60–73.

three of these mysteries affirm the same thing, that "God has imparted himself to us through Jesus Christ in his Spirit as he is in himself, so that the inexpressible nameless mystery which reigns in us and over us should be in itself the immediate blessedness of the spirit which knows, and transforms itself into love."[8]

The quality of mystery belongs originally and primarily to God. By virtue of our transcendental orientation to God we also partake in the mystery. We are inescapably and fundamentally oriented toward the absolute, holy mystery of God. This transcendental orientation to God is the a priori condition of possibility for every act of knowledge and freedom, and so is an inescapable part of human experience and a fundamental element of human nature. Every human experience is a transcendental experience in which we reach toward the unlimited horizon of the holy mystery of God. We always live in the presence of and are related to this absolute mystery, even when we are not directly conscious of it and even when we are absorbed with the particular and comprehensible realities of everyday life.

A secret ingredient of human life is the grasp of the incomprehensibility of God, "before which we can only fall dumb in adoration; before which and towards which we exist, whether we wish to or not; being able only to choose whether to accept this exposure to the mystery *per se*, entering into it in believing liberty, or whether to repress it skeptically."[9] We can see here how Rahner could think that we are made for worship. We are inescapably oriented to the absolute mystery of God, and, whether we acknowledge it or not, our lives are filled with this holy mystery which has drawn near to us. The liturgy is a symbolic expression of our fundamental acceptance of the absolute mystery, and of the absolute mystery's free and forgiving acceptance of us. Worship is an experience of interpersonal communion with the absolute, holy mystery.

8. Ibid., 73.
9. Karl Rahner, "The Theological Dimension of the Question About Man," TI 17 (New York: Crossroad, 1981) 61.

In our "natural" experiences of transcendence, the absolute mystery of God is present to us as the horizon which we can only approach asymptotically, ever drawing nearer to it but never surpassing it. The heart of the Christian message, however, is that God has not remained the distant horizon of human transcendence but has graciously drawn near to us as free and forgiving love. We live in a world that is already, but not yet fully, redeemed. We never experience our transcendence, therefore, as purely natural and ungraced. Our experience of transcendence is always an experience of graced transcendence. The transcendence we actually experience has been radically transformed by God's self-communication, which is always present at least as an invitation made to our freedom. Nor do we ever experience the goal of our transcendence as merely remote and unreachable. The horizon that we actually experience is one that also gives itself directly to us. We can only speculate about what a natural experience of our transcendence, in which the goal of our transcendence appeared simply and completely as the ungraspable horizon, would be like. The horizon has in fact drawn near to us. That does not mean we do not experience the absolute mystery as a horizon that is always just out of our reach. Everything we have already said about an experience of the supreme horizon being the secret ingredient of every fully human experience is true. But Christians also claim that we experience that horizon as a horizon which has made itself immediately present to us as the fulfillment of our transcendence. The absolute horizon is and remains a horizon, but it simultaneously is and remains a horizon that has drawn near. In other words, the paradox is that at one and the same time, God remains the utterly transcendent God but communicates himself to us in all our historical and material particularity through the experience of grace.[10]

10. The primary sources for Rahner's theology of grace are Karl Rahner, "Concerning the Relationship Between Nature and Grace," TI 1 (Baltimore: Helicon, 1961) 297–317; "Some Implications of the Scholastic Concept of Uncreated Grace," TI 1 (Baltimore: Helicon, 1961) 319–346; "Nature and Grace," TI 4 (New York: Crossroad, 1982), 165–88; *Foundations of Christian*

Rahner thinks, therefore, that grace is best understood not as the communication of a finite created gift separate from God, but as the *self*-communication of God.[11] Grace is not a gift *from* God, but the gift *of* God. Rahner's studies of the New Testament provided the foundation for this approach. When the New Testament writers use the term *theos*, they mean the first person of the Trinity, the Father. In the New Testament, *theos* does not mean each of the three divine persons, or the divine nature common to all three divine persons together. That would be the usage that was later favored by Latin Trinitarian theology. The New Testament usage of *theos*, the usage that was adopted by Greek theology, is one in which this term signifies the first person of the Trinity alone.[12] Rahner follows the same pattern: When he speaks about the self-communication of God, he has God as the unoriginated, absolute holy mystery in mind. The claim made by the writers of the New Testament is precisely that the utterly transcendent God has indeed dwelt among us and

Faith, 116–133; "Grace": 2, "Theological," *Encyclopedia of Theology: The Concise Sacramentum Mundi*, 587–595; "Grace": 3, "Structure of 'De Gratia,'" ibid., 595–598; and "Revelation": 2, "God's Self-Communication," ibid., 1466–1468. *See also* George Vass, *The Mystery of Man and the Foundations of a Theological System*, 59–116; John Cawte, "Karl Rahner's Conception of God's Self-communication to Man," *Heythrop Journal* 25 (1984) 260–271; Joseph F. Sica, *God So Loved the World* (Washington: University Press of America, 1981); B. van der Heijden, *Karl Rahner: Darstellung und kritik seiner Grundposition* (Einsiedeln: Johannes Verlag, 1973); Klaus Fischer, "Kritik der 'Grundpositionen'? Kritische Anmerkungen zu B. van der Heijden's Buch über Karl Rahner," *ZKTh* 99 (1977) 74–89; Kenneth D. Eberhard, "Karl Rahner and the Supernatural Existential," *Thought* 46 (1971) 537–561; Traugott Koch, "Natur und Gnade. Zur neueren Diskussion," *KuD* 16 (1970) 171–187; Lee H. Yearley, "Karl Rahner on the Relation of Nature and Grace," *Canadian Journal of Theology* 16 (1970) 219–231; Thomas J. Motherway, "Supernatural Existential," *Chicago Studies* 4 (1965) 79–103; Carl J. Peter, "The Position of Karl Rahner Regarding the Supernatural: A Comparative Study of Nature and Grace," *PCTSA* 20 (1965) 81–94; and William J. Hill, "Uncreated Grace: A Critique of Karl Rahner," *Thomist* 27 (1963) 333–356.

11. On Rahner's different uses of "self-communication" *(Selbstmitteilung)*, "self-emptying" *(Selbstentäusserung)*, "self-expression" *(Selbstäusserung)*, and "self-utterance" *(Selbstaussage)*, see John Cawte, "Karl Rahner's Conception of God's Self-communication to Man," 263–264.

12. K. Rahner, *"Theos* in the New Testament," 125–148.

continues to dwell among us. The God who is given to us in the history of salvation and the experience of grace is the God who is wholly other. This is why the incarnation and grace are mysteries in the strict sense of the word: because it is the absolutely transcendent God who is communicated to the historical and material world in them.

Furthermore, Rahner concluded that St. Paul's understanding of grace is one in which the *pneuma hagion* itself dwells in us and leads us. For Paul, our inner sanctification is first and foremost a communication of the personal Spirit of God (what Scholastic theology calls "uncreated grace"). Every created grace, every way of being *pneumatikos*, is seen by Paul as a consequence and manifestation of the possession of this uncreated grace. The notion of God's own indwelling in those who are sanctified is also present in the Johannine theology of grace. Likewise, the Fathers (especially the Greek Fathers) see the created gifts of grace as a consequence of God's substantial communication to those who are justified.[13] The self-communication of God, in other words, should not be reduced to the effects which that self-communication has upon us. For example, grace transforms us, empowers and enlightens us, and makes us more loving, gentle, and wise. But all these marvelous gifts are effects of the original and more marvelous gift: the actual self-communication *of* God. Since the effects of the basic gift are more immediately apparent and comprehensible than the basic gift of God's self-communication itself is, we are easily distracted by them and frequently mistake them for the substance of grace. The substance of the experience of grace, however, is the indwelling of the Spirit of God.

In the course of such studies, Rahner came to believe that the traditional theology of grace did not do justice to the New Testament's way of speaking. Traditional theology viewed sanctifying grace as a created modification of the human soul, whereas the Scriptures speak of it as the gift of God's Spirit. Grace had come to be seen primarily as a gift *from* God, rather than as the gift *of*

13. K. Rahner, "Some Implications of the Scholastic Concept of Uncreated Grace," 320–324.

God. For Rahner, the basic problem was that many theologians saw grace as some-*thing* that is produced through efficient causality. Grace was identified with some change that took place in believers. Consequently, grace was seen as something separate from God, and as something made by God. But the notion of efficient causality is a better explanation of what happens in the order of creation, for there the infinite God brings finite beings, which are wholly other than God, into existence. The Scriptures, however, imply that there is a different kind of causality involved in the order of grace, a kind of causality that approaches that which we know as formal causality. Rahner calls this process of grace "quasi-formal" causality. It is like formal causality because God is actually communicated to us, yet it is unlike formal causality in that we do not in the process become God.[14] We participate in God through grace, and so we are transformed and become like God, but we do not ever become God. God's self-communication is unlike anything else in our experience, and it can never be completely explained. Christians claim that they know such a process is possible because they believe it is what has happened in the incarnation and in grace.

In the process of grace, God does not merely give us some created and indirect share of the divine being through efficient causality. Through a quasi-formal causality, God is really and in the strictest sense of the word given to us. Grace is not a finite thing, even though the effects in us of the self-communication of God may be understood as finite and created realities. Properly speaking, grace is the divine *self*-communication in which God is communicated to us. As such, grace is not something provisional nor is it merely a means to salvation or a substitute for salvation. Since grace is God's self-communication, it is really salvation itself.[15] For what would salvation be if not the fulfillment of our essential openness to God through the self-gift of God?

In receiving the self-communication of God, therefore, we do not cease to be human. On the contrary, God's self-communication

14. Ibid., 329–331; *Foundations of Christian Faith*, 120–122.
15. K. Rahner, "Concerning the Relationship Between Nature and Grace," 307–308; "Nature and Grace," 177; and *Foundations of Christian Faith*, 117–120.

realizes our deepest human potential. We are spirit-in-the-world: radically conditioned by matter and history but also radically open to the absolute holy mystery. Our openness to the utterly transcendent is what is most essentially and characteristically human about us. We are that part of the world that is defined by its ability to enter into an interpersonal communion with God. Our deepest potential as human beings is to hear a word from God that would not simply be a word about God, but would really be the word *of* God. We are those finite beings that have room within our hearts to welcome the infinite God as God. Our salvation is the complete fulfillment of all this potential through the self-communication of God. That is why the end of salvation is referred to as the beatific vision; our face-to-face communion with God. This communion begins in grace, by which we are gradually transformed and become like God. In this way, we become fully and completely human. The paradox of salvation is that the more we become like God through the gift of grace, the more human we become. Our humanization takes place in direct, not inverse, proportion to our divinization. Our humanity is not diminished by the gift of God but becomes more and more what it is meant to be: the place where the world and God become fully and personally present to each other. God does not become any less God by being communicated to us in grace, nor do we become any less human by receiving the gift of God.

In grace, therefore, the absolute holy mystery, which is experienced as the horizon of our natural transcendence, is communicated to us. This does not mean that God is no longer experienced as completely ineffable and incomprehensible. The God who is communicated to us in grace remains God and so remains absolute mystery. Grace is the self-communication of God *as* the absolute mystery, which remains absolute mystery. The holy mystery which is the horizon of human transcendence is no longer distant and aloof but becomes immediate and near. Grace is the event of the nearness of the abiding mystery.

"Divine self-communication means, then, that God can communicate himself in his own reality to what is not divine without ceasing to be infinite reality and absolute mystery, and without man ceasing to be a finite existent different from God. This self-communication does not cancel out or deny what was said earlier about the presence of God as the absolute mystery which is essentially incomprehensible. Even in grace and in the immediate vision of God, God remains God, that is, the first and the ultimate measure which can be measured by nothing else. He remains the mystery which alone is self-evident, the term of man's highest act, the term by which this act is borne and made possible. God remains the holy One who is really accessible only in worship.''[16]

THE WORLD AS GRACED

The previous section focused on our understanding of *what* grace is: that it is the gift of God rather than a gift from God. This section will look at the issue of *when* and *where* grace is to be found. In the passage just cited, Rahner claims that the God who is graciously communicated to us is really accessible only in worship. But Rahner also thinks that worship, and the experience of grace, are not confined to explicitly religious events. Worship takes place throughout human history. And the gift of God's self-communication is always and everywhere present in the world and in human experience, at least as an offer. The whole world has been permeated by the grace of God.

Rahner thinks that there are two models for understanding the relationship between God's self-communication in grace and the world. The first model is the one which dominated post-Tridentine theology. It portrays the presence of grace in the world primarily as an intervention of God at definite points in space and time. God's grace is given to a world that is normally deprived of it. The presence of grace is restricted to very limited circumstances and events. Ordinarily, our experiences of the world are experiences of the absence, not the presence, of grace. Experiences of grace are necessarily extraordinary and highly unusual events. The world is primarily secular both because nature is by definition ungraced and because of the inherited sinful state of our history. If God's self-communication is supposed

16. K. Rahner, *Foundations of Christian Faith*, 119–120.

nevertheless to be present in the world, this presence must take place as an intervention of God in certain discrete events. The grace of God does not really belong in the world.[17]

The concept of nature can be given the widest variety of meanings. Within the first model, "nature" generally denotes an abstract construction of those elements necessary to define what the world is when it is considered apart from grace. Such a definition of pure nature supposedly demonstrates the gratuity of grace, because the definition of human nature includes a kind of natural integrity that demands nothing beyond itself in order for it to be fulfilled. Grace is not demanded by human nature for its fulfillment. Human nature can get along without grace, and so grace is not something that God is required to give us. Moreover, this concept of nature can be used to precisely determine the qualities that are due to grace. The attributes of the natural person can be subtracted from those of the graced person, and we will be left with a concrete account of those characteristics that are due to grace. Nature and grace are seen in this first model, then, as two distinct entities. The image of the world it suggests is that of a two-story house where grace and nature are on separate levels, grace building upon nature but never really belonging to it or penetrating it.

The first model is not without its merits, chief of which is its ability to protect the gratuity of grace. But is this the only way in which the idea that grace is a gift that we can neither expect nor demand can be defended? This model is based on the implicit assumption that grace can be an absolutely free gift of God only if it becomes present in a secular and sinful world to which it is normally denied. Grace is a gift because it is something we do not ordinarily receive, nor do we have any right to expect it. Our typical, everyday experience is of a world generally devoid of grace, not only because it is natural but also because it is a fallen world. In the first model, those events in which grace does become available, such as salvation history, the Church, and the

17. K. Rahner, "Considerations on the Active Role of the Person in the Sacramental Event," TI 14 (New York: Seabury, 1976) 161–170; "On the Theology of Worship," TI 19 (New York: Crossroad, 1983) 141–146.

sacraments, are important precisely because they provide access to that gift of grace that is normally absent. And they are necessary precisely because they are the only means we have of acquiring the extraordinary gift of grace.[18]

Rahner's own model of the operation of grace in the world starts out from the assumption that it is not necessary for the world to be normally deprived of grace in order for grace to be a gift. We do not need to think that the experience of grace must be something foreign and unfamiliar, something given only to a few on relatively rare occasions, for it to be remarkable. Grace is not less of a gift because it is universally available. The fact that the self-gift of God is lavished upon us so extravagantly does not make grace any less marvelous, extraordinary, unexpected, or undeserved. The self-communication of God will still be a gift, no matter how profligate God might be with it. If anything, the gratuity of grace is enhanced by the generosity of God.

Rahner assumes, therefore, that the "secular" world is from the outset always encompassed and permeated with the grace of God's self-communication. God's self-communication is present in our world and our history in two forms: as an offer made to our freedom and as the acceptance or rejection by our freedom of this offer. The presence of grace as an offer is the most pervasive, and in some ways the most minimal, way in which the self-communication of God is present in the world, but it is a real presence of grace nonetheless. The offer of God's self-communication is never withdrawn, no matter how hardened or resistent we might be to this invitation. And the self-communication of God is offered not only to the human community but to the entire universe as well. God invites every part of the cosmos to enter into communion with the absolute mystery according to its own capacity. The material world cannot enter into an interpersonal relationship with God, but it can be united with God as something loved by God.

In the second form of the presence of grace, grace becomes more marvelously and manifestly present when it is freely ac-

18. K. Rahner, "Concerning the Relationship Between Nature and Grace," 297–310; and "Nature and Grace," 165–173.

cepted by human beings. The most complete and explicit presence of grace in the world comes when grace is freely and fully accepted in the total surrender of a human person to God. But even the free and perverse rejection of God reveals the presence of grace. The unconditional love of God is never withdrawn from even the most obstinate sinner. Even those persons whose condemnation has become irreversible are loved by God, and in this sense they continue to experience grace, albeit as something rejected. It is not an experience of grace that leads them to communion with God, and therefore to salvation, but it is still an experience of grace.

In either case, whether as an offer or as an offer accepted or rejected, the self-communication of God is present always and everywhere.[19]

"The world is permeated by the grace of God. . . . The world is constantly and ceaselessly possessed by grace from its innermost roots, from the innermost personal center of the spiritual subject. It is constantly and ceaselessly sustained and moved by God's self-bestowal even prior to the question (admittedly crucial) of how creaturely freedom reacts to this 'engracing' of the world and of the spiritual creature as already given and 'offered,' the question, in other words, of whether this creaturely freedom accepts the grace to its salvation or closes itself to it to its perdition. Whether the world gives the impression, so far as our superficial everyday experience is concerned, of being imbued with grace in this way, or whether it constantly seems to give the lie to this state of being permeated by God's grace which it has, this in no sense alters the fact that it is so."[20]

Our superficial experience of the world does perhaps correspond more evidently to the first model of nature and grace. Most often, God's absence is much more painfully obvious than God's presence. The world frequently appears to be much more deeply permeated by sin and evil and suffering than by the gracious love of God. But Christians claim that the world is not as it may

19. K. Rahner, "Nature and Grace," 179–181.
20. K. Rahner, "Considerations on the Active Role of the Person in the Sacramental Event," 166–167.

appear to be. The world is in fact ceaselessly endowed with God's grace. The world as "nature" is not a self-sufficient, independent reality to which grace is subsequently added by God. God lovingly sustains the natural world precisely as the potential recipient of the divine self-communication. From the outset, grace is the innermost center of this nature. Grace has been offered to the world from the very beginning of its existence by virtue of the fact that the world is created as a potential recipient of grace. Consequently, nature as it actually exists is never purely and simply secular, it is always oriented toward and endowed with God. Those realities in which the presence of grace is explicitly expressed, such as the events of salvation history, the Church, and the sacraments, are important and necessary precisely because they do explicitly manifest the grace that quietly permeates the world.[21]

This is not a form of intrinsicism, where nature is so oriented toward grace and so saturated with grace as to be completely indistinguishable from it. Some concept of pure nature is necessary to affirm the gratuity of grace. The concept of pure nature provides the background against which grace is seen as unexacted and freely given. But Rahner says that when it is defined in the theological sense, nature is a remainder concept (*Restbegriff*). It is a reality that must be postulated as that which is left over in us when we subtract God's ever-present offer of grace from who we are as concrete human beings. This pure nature remains a postulate and cannot be concretely distinguished from grace. Herein lies a basic difference between Rahner's model and the first model. The first model is confident of its ability to precisely and explicitly distinguish the natural from the supernatural, whereas Rahner maintains that the nature that is actually available to us is always imbued with the grace of God. Since nature has in fact been graced, we are never given an experience of pure nature, but only experiences of nature as graced. The only nature we know and experience is a graced nature, and so we can only

21. K. Rahner, "Nature and Grace," 182–185.

speculate in the vaguest and most hesitant terms about what a life without grace would concretely be like.[22]

The point that the world is permeated with grace has everything to do with the notion of the universal salvific will of God. That God wills the salvation of every human being is axiomatic for Rahner's theology of grace. In this context, he never tires of quoting 1 Timothy 2:4, ''(God our Savior) desires everyone to be saved and to come to the knowledge of the truth.'' For Rahner, this is the very heart of the Christian message. We live in an objective situation of salvation in which we are convinced that God really wills the salvation of everyone, while at the same time the future salvation of any individual is still in the balance. The process of salvation history has never been a matter of bringing about a will to save in God. God has always willed everyone's salvation. The problem has been to get the human community to freely accept the salvation offered by God. The events of salvation history, which were fulfilled in the Christ event, did not bring about a will to save in God that had not existed previously or would not have existed otherwise. God did not choose the people of Israel at the expense of the Gentiles but so that all might be saved. And God continues to offer salvation to all. We can be certain that everyone is freely invited to enter into communion with God. What will happen in the case of any particular individual remains uncertain, however, because that will depend on the individual's free acceptance or rejection of God.[23]

22. K. Rahner, *Foundations of Christian Faith*, 123–125; ''Nature and Grace,'' 185–188; and ''Concerning the Relationship Between Nature and Grace,'' 310–317. Note that Rahner uses the term ''nature'' in a different way in his discussion of freedom, where it means ''everything which is presupposed for the existential self-determination of human freedom as the condition of its possibility. It is immaterial whether it is the simple, finite reality of creation or the unmerited gift bestowed upon this nature in its own proper way as the 'being' of man.'' *See* Karl Rahner, ''Experience of the Spirit and Existential Commitment,'' TI 16 (New York: Crossroad, 1983) 28.

23. *See* Karl Rahner, ''Salvation'': 1, ''Universal Salvific Will,'' *Encyclopedia of Theology: The Concise Sacramentum Mundi*, 1499–1504; ''Membership of the Church According to the Teaching of Pius XII's Encyclical 'Mystici Corporis Christi,' '' TI 2 (Baltimore: Helicon, 1963) 1–88; ''The Christian Among Unbelieving Relations,'' TI 3 (New York: Crossroad, 1982) 355–372; ''Chris-

(This is the starting point of Rahner's famous theory of the anonymous Christian.[24])

Rahner's notion of the supernatural existential is a necessary implication of God's universal salvific will. For Rahner, an existential is a characteristic or capacity of human existence that makes it specifically human and distinguishes it from other modes of existence. We have many existentials, among which the supernatural existential has to do with our being oriented toward the immediate vision of the absolute mystery of God. The supernatural existential is a precondition of our historical situation and not of our essence as spirit. Our essence as spirit only orients us toward the ever-distant, absolute horizon. It means that in the real, historical order in which we live, our human nature is always more than just "pure nature." We are always also characterized by our supernatural orientation. To be human is to be invited into that interpersonal communion with God which is our salvation. Even before we might be transformed by grace, we are already subject to the universal salvific will of God and obligated to pursue the fulfillment of our deepest potential: union with God. This situation is prior to our free self-realization. That is to say, this is something that is given with our human nature; it is not a situation we can choose. The supernatural existential is not merely an external circumstance, nor does it exist only in

tianity and the Non-Christian Religions," TI 5 (New York: Crossroad, 1983) 115–134; "Church, Churches and Religions," TI 10 (New York: Seabury, 1977) 30–49; "The One Christ and the Universality of Salvation," TI 16 (New York: Crossroad, 1983) 199–224; "On the Importance of the Non-Christian Religions for Salvation" TI 18 (New York: Crossroad, 1983) 288–295; and "Christianity": 1, "The Essence of Christianity," *Encyclopedia of Theology: The Concise* Sacramentum Mundi, 188–202.

24. See Karl Rahner, "Anonymous Christians," TI 6 (New York: Crossroad, 1982) 390–398; "Observations on the Problem of the 'Anonymous Christian,'" TI 14 (New York: Seabury, 1976) 280–294; and "Anonymous and Explicit Faith," TI 16 (New York: Crossroad, 1983) 52–59. *See also* Karl-Heinz Weger, "Überlegungen zum 'anonymen Christentum,'" *Wagnis Theologie*, hrsg. H. Vorgrimler (Freiburg: Herder, 1979) 499–510; and Klaus Riesenhuber, "Rahner's 'Anonymous Christian,'" *Christian Witness in the Secular City*, ed. E. J. Morgan (Chicago: Loyola University Press, 1970) 142–154.

God's intentions, but is a real ontological modification of our concrete, historical nature. Since it is added to our nature by God's grace, it can be described as supernatural, although in the real, historical world in which we live it is never lacking. Even when we are in sin we are continually affected by this situation.[25]

The supernatural existential is not merely our essential openness to God. It is an a priori condition by means of which we are concretely disposed for encounter with God through God's self-communication. It is a gift to our nature and not simply a potential of that nature, and so it shares in the gratuity of grace. The immediate vision of God is not owed to our nature and, therefore, it is something that can be frustrated in us; we could exist without it. Both our potential for immediate, interpersonal communion with God and the fulfillment of that potential are free gifts of God. To say otherwise would mean that this grace would no longer be grace but would be demanded by human nature. The supernatural existential is an essential element of God's self-communication to us in grace. And so Rahner says, "This antecedent self-communication of God which is prior to man's freedom means nothing else but that the spirit's transcendental movement in knowledge and love towards the absolute mystery is borne by God himself in his self-communication in such a way that this movement has its term and its source not in the holy mystery as eternally distant and as a goal which can only be reached asymptotically, but rather in the God of absolute closeness and immediacy."[26]

As is the case with the other elements of our transcendental constitution, we do not have an individual, a posteriori, and categorical experience of the supernatural existential. It is an ele-

25. K. Rahner, *Foundations of Christian Faith*, 126–133; "Existence": 2, "The Existential," B, "Theological," *Encyclopedia of Theology: The Concise Sacramentum Mundi*, 494–495; "Existential, übernatürliches," *Lexikon für Theologie und Kirche* 3, hrsg. J. Höfer + K. Rahner (Freiburg: Herder, 1959) col. 1301; and Karl Rahner and Herbert Vorgrimler, *Dictionary of Theology*, 2nd ed. (New York: Crossroad, 1981) 163–164.
26. K. Rahner, *Foundations of Christian Faith*, 129.

ment within our transcendental experiences and is not encountered by us as an clear and distinct object. The most we can do is to point to it by reflecting on our experience of grace. Therefore, the supernatural existential can be just as easily overlooked, denied, or falsely interpreted as any other dimension of our transcendental experience.

Grace, then, is available always and everywhere, at least as an offer. Our transcendental orientation to the absolute, holy mystery of God is universally graced by God's self-communication. The fact that grace is always present, that our concrete "natural" existence is one that is always endowed with grace, does not detract from either the supernatural character of that grace or its gratuity. The love of God does not become less a miracle by the fact that it is given to everyone at least as an offer. So Rahner says: "Grace is always the free action of divine love which is only 'at the disposal' of man precisely in so far as he is at the disposal of this divine love. One must indeed always remember that God is not diminished by our becoming greater. And in the last resort, Christianity is not the religion whose basic attitude is fear of its going to our head—and not into our grateful heart—if we extol the greatness to which God has raised man in order that he might praise God."[27]

27. K. Rahner, "Nature and Grace," 177.

Chapter Three

The Experience of God

We have seen that we are spirit-in-the-world, and so that we are essentially and inescapably oriented to the absolute mystery of God. And we have seen that the absolute mystery ceaselessly and universally offers its self-gift to us. In other words, we are open to the possibility of a genuine experience of God, and God is graciously made available for such an experience. The sort of personal communion with God presupposed by our idea of worship, therefore, is reasonable. Human experience of God in which we do not cease to be human and God does not cease to be God is not inconceivable. Our theology of worship will have everything to do with our understanding of how, when, and where such experiences of God take place.

THE CONCEPT OF EXPERIENCE

Before we can explore what we mean by the experience of God, we need to clarify the concept of experience. For Rahner, experience is one of the ways we grasp the objects of knowledge. Experience is a way of knowing, and whatever we discover about experiential knowledge in general will help illuminate the dynamics of the experience of God. What happens in our experience of God is comparable to what happens in our typical experiences of such basic human realities as joy, faithfulness, trust, and love. But our experience of God is also atypical, and it cannot simply be lumped together with these other experiences because the object of this experience, the absolute mystery of God, is unique. God is radically different from any other object of experience, and so our experience of God will be unlike anything else. Nonetheless, our basic experiential knowledge of God does have something in common with our other experiences, especially our basic experience of ourselves.[1]

Experiential knowledge is best understood in relation to conceptual knowledge. For Rahner, experience is that type of knowledge that arises from the direct reception of an impression from an internal or external reality that lies outside our free control. Experience is a more passive way of knowing something than is conceptualization. When we know things conceptually, we actively categorize them according to our perspectives and methods, and we deliberately subject them to critical investigation and analysis. When we know something conceptually, we fit it into our intellectual horizons. Conceptual knowledge strives to master its objects by comprehending their relationships to the whole universe of meaning. When we experience something, however, we receive it with a minimal amount of analysis or examination. Experiential knowledge does not try to master its ob-

---

1. Karl Rahner, "Reflections on the Experience of Grace," TI 3 (New York: Crossroad, 1982) 86–90; "The Experience of God Today," TI 11 (New York: Crossroad, 1982) 149–165; "Experience of Self and Experience of God," TI 13 (New York: Crossroad, 1983) 122–132; "Experience of the Spirit and Existential Commitment," TI 16 (New York: Crossroad, 1983) 24–34; "Experience of Transcendence from the Standpoint of Catholic Dogmatics," TI 18 (New York: Crossroad, 1983) 173–188; "Experience of the Holy Spirit," TI 18 (New York: Crossroad, 1983) 189–210; and "Religious Feeling Inside and Outside the Church," TI 17 (New York: Crossroad, 1981) 231–238. See also James Bacik, Apologetics and the Eclipse of Mystery: Mystagogy According to Karl Rahner (Notre Dame: University of Notre Dame Press, 1980) 20–38; Klaus P. Fischer, Gotteserfahrung: Mystagogie in der Theologie Karl Rahners und in der Theologie der Befreiung (Mainz: Matthias-Grünewald Verlag, 1986); Herbert Vorgrimler, "Gotteserfahrung im Alltag. Der Beitrag Karl Rahners zu Spiritualität und Mystik," Vor dem Geheimnis Gottes den Menschen verstehen. Karl Rahner zum 80. Geburtstag, hrsg. K. Lehman (München, Verlag Schnell und Steiner, 1984) 62–78; Paul Weß, "Wie kann der Mensch Gott erfahren? Eine Überlegung zur Theologie Karl Rahners," Theologisches Jahrbuch (1982) 64–69 (and in ZKTh 102 [1980] 343–348); Erich Schrofner, "Gnade und Erfahrung bei Karl Rahner und Leonardo Boff. Zwei Wege gegenwärtiger Gnadentheologie," Geist und Leben 53 (1980) 266–280; J. Norman King, "The Experience of God in the Theology of Karl Rahner," Thought 53 (1978) 174–202; and Denis Edwards, "Experience of God and Explicit Faith: A Comparison of John of the Cross and Karl Rahner," Thomist 46 (1982) 33–74.

jects or fit them within precise and limited categories. Nor does experience dissect its objects. On the contrary, it strives to be consciously and completely open to the object in its totality. Experiential knowledge attempts to be immediately present to, and uncritically aware of, something that lies beyond our control.

The differences between experiential knowledge and conceptual knowledge emerge when we compare the ways we experience and conceptualize ourselves. Our conceptual grasp of ourselves comes from stepping back and actively analyzing ourselves. This happens, for example, if we take the time to categorize our likes and dislikes or our strengths and weaknesses. When we take such personal inventories, we attempt to define who we are and calculate how we fit into the human community and the world. But we also have another way of knowing ourselves: experiencing ourselves. Through such basic self-experience, which to some extent comes to us whether we seek it or not, we have a much more immediate grasp of ourselves than we are ever able to put into words. In such experience, we are as immediately present to ourselves as possible, and we know ourselves more completely and accurately than we are able to conceptually articulate. When we know ourselves through such experiences, we are aware of ourselves without defining ourselves.

While experience and conceptualization are different, they are intimately related to one another. Within this relationship, experience is logically prior to conceptual knowledge. Conceptual knowledge can obviously precede experience temporally. For instance, we can acquire a conceptual understanding of love before we have had any experience of it. Ultimately, however, our conceptual knowledge of realities such as love, or fear, or ourselves attempts to interpret our own and other people's experiences of these realities, and in this sense, experience is an a priori way of knowing.[2]

---

2. Karl Rahner and Herbert Vorgrimler, *Dictionary of Theology*, 2nd ed. (New York: Crossroad, 1981) 164; K. Rahner, "The Experience of God Today," 149–152; "Experience of Self and Experience of God," 122–124; and "Dogmatic Reflections on the Knowledge and Self-consciousness of Christ," TI 5 (New York: Crossroad, 1983) 193–215.

Since experience is the direct passive reception of impressions of a reality, it gives us a kind of knowledge that is more immediate and complete than our conceptual grasp of that reality. For example, our experience of ourselves is more basic and immediate than our conceptual knowledge of ourselves. We know more about ourselves through our experience of ourselves than we are able to express in conceptual terms. Conceptual knowledge, then, never completely captures any basic experience. The knowledge that we have in an experience is so direct and comprehensive that it is impossible to express it fully in conceptual terms. This is why we can communicate our conceptual knowledge *about* something to someone else, but we can never communicate our experience *of* something to another person. For example, we can communicate a great deal of information about ourselves to another person, but we never fully communicate the breadth and depth of our self-experience. We can never give our experience of our ourselves to another person wholly and exactly; we can only point to it. At best, our conceptual grasp of the objects of our basic experiences is always incomplete.

Conceptual knowledge about the objects of our basic experiences is limited further by the fact that we frequently do not reflect upon our experiences. Sometimes, this is simply because we overlook them; at other times, because we deliberately suppress them. We constantly have experiences that we overlook because our attention is directed elsewhere, and we frequently have experiences that for any number of reasons we choose to deny. Such dynamics seriously limit our conceptual grasp of the objects of our experiences. Furthermore, even when we do deliberately reflect upon our experiences, our interpretations can simply be mistaken. We are all too painfully aware, for example, that our conceptual interpretations of ourselves can be very inaccurate. Despite the best of intentions and considerable effort at self-examination, we often discover that who we think we are is considerably different from who we experience ourselves to be.

This does not mean that experiential knowledge and conceptual knowledge are hopelessly separated from one another. Experience always involves at least a certain incipient and rudimentary process of conceptualization. The transition from experience to conceptual knowledge may be very difficult, but it is nonetheless often successful. For example, much of what we are able to articulate about ourselves is true to our experience of ourselves. When this transition from experience to conceptual knowledge is successful, it can in turn help us to be clearly attentive to, and more deeply aware of, our basic experiences. Rahner says that an experience of something can be "accepted more profoundly, more purely, and with greater freedom when we achieve a knowledge of its true nature and its implications at the explicitly conscious level."[3]

Finally, experience is inescapable in a way in which conceptual knowledge is not. Again, this is because experience is a direct and immediate reception of impressions from an object. Conceptual knowledge requires a significant amount of active participation on our part. The extent of our conceptual grasp of anything is directly related to the amount of effort we have freely given to analyzing it. But experience is not within our control to anywhere near the same degree. We may ignore, suppress, or deny our basic experiences, but we still have those experiences. For example, we may not have a reflective, conceptual knowledge of ourselves, but we cannot avoid experiencing ourselves. We may have little or no conceptual knowledge of something, but that does not necessarily mean that we do not have any experiential knowledge of it. In fact, we frequently have experiences of realities about which we do not have clear and adequate conceptual knowledge.

THE EXPERIENCE OF GOD

There is something inescapable about any human experience, but a distinguishing feature of our basic experience of God is that it is absolutely inescapable. It is possible that someone might not have an experience of such things as love, hate, sorrow, or joy. But it is impossible for anyone not to have a basic experience of God. Everyone has an experience of the absolute mystery, "whether consciously or unconsciously, whether sup-

3. K. Rahner, "The Experience of God Today," 152.

pressed or accepted, whether rightly or wrongly interpreted, or whatever the way in which it is present."[4]

The experience of God is utterly inescapable because we experience God whenever we experience our transcendence. Whenever we know or choose anything, we experience the absolute mystery. We are not normally aware of this; it is as difficult to catch ourselves in the act of experiencing God as it is to catch ourselves in the act of any other transcendental experience. But every conscious and fully human experience of our daily lives involves a secret transcendental experience of God. In the "natural" state of our transcendence, the absolute mystery is vaguely present as a distant and aloof horizon, which we can only approach asymptotically. Our natural transcendental orientation to the holy mystery, however, has been universally graced by God's self-communication. Through this grace, an immediate experience of God, which is always mediated by our historicity and materiality, becomes possible for us. The distant and aloof horizon of natural transcendence becomes the God who is near and accessible to everyone as unconditional love and forgiveness. But the God who draws near in grace continues to be absolute mystery. The universality of God's self-communication does not of itself mean that the presence of God is revealed any more distinctly and explicitly than it would be if our transcendental experiences were purely "natural." In every experience of our graced transcendence, we are given an experience of the God who is eternally open to us and eternally hidden from us.[5]

Being an experience of the absolute, holy mystery, the experience of God is different from any other experience. It is not, for instance, given to us in addition to other experiences. The experience of God lies hidden within every human experience. We cannot experience anything without simultaneously experiencing the absolute mystery. Our explicit experience of any historical, material object is always also an implicit experience of the utterly

4. Ibid., 150. *See also* K. Rahner, "Experience of the Holy Spirit," 195.
5. K. Rahner, "The Experience of God Today," 153; "Experience of Self and Experience of God," 123–124; "Reflections on the Experience of Grace," 86–87; "Experience of the Spirit and Existential Commitment," 27–29; and "Experience of the Holy Spirit," 195–199.

transcendent and gracious God. This experience of the holy mystery should not, therefore, be thought of as one particular experience among many other basic experiences. We do not sometimes have experiences of love, fear, ourselves, or anything else and then also have experiences of God. The basic, original experience of God, on the contrary, is "the ultimate depths and the radical essence of *every* spiritual and personal experience (of love, faithfulness, hope and so on), and thereby precisely constitutes also the ultimate unity and totality of experience, in which the person as spiritual possesses himself and is made over to himself."[6]

This is why the experience of God is so completely inescapable. We cannot help experiencing God, however dimly, at some level of our being whenever we experience anything. The experience of the absolute mystery is not given only to those who are considered great saints or mystics, to those who have been taught about God, or to those who interpret their lives in religious categories. Even those who would expressly deny it, implicitly experience God.[7] Rahner says:

"It precisely does *not* depend upon whether we do or do not call the reality to which it refers 'God,' whether or not we express the experience to ourselves in conceptual terms in a theoretical statement about God, whether the individual concerned freely identifies himself with his experience or denies it, suppresses it, or leaves it unexplored. The experience of God which we are pointing to here is not some subsequent emotional reaction to doctrinal instruction about the existence and nature of God which we received from without and at the theoretical level. Rather it is prior to any such teaching, underlies it, and has to be there already for it to be made intelligible at all. This experience of God is not the privilege of the individual 'mystic,' but is present in every man even though the process of reflecting upon it varies greatly from one individual to another in terms of force and clarity."[8]

6. K. Rahner, "The Experience of God Today," 154.
7. K. Rahner, "Experience of Self and Experience of God," 124–132.
8. K. Rahner, "The Experience of God Today," 153.

Normally, we experience God without being aware that we are doing so. Because the experience of the absolute mystery is so basic and inescapable, it does not strike us as irresistibly as most ordinary experiences do. The ordinary experiences of daily life come and go, and so they stand out from one another and from the rest of life. But the fact that we continually experience God makes it very difficult for us to be explicitly conscious of experiencing God. We take our experience of the absolute mystery for granted and overlook it, precisely because it is the most pervasive and unavoidable human experience. Our chronic inability to see God in the midst of ordinary daily life is not a confirmation of God's absence but a consequence of God's radical presence. The experience of the absolute mystery usually lies far in the background, behind the other experiences with which it is given. The one experience in life that should, theoretically, be the most apparent to us is in fact the most hidden.

This basic experience of God is prior to and more fundamental than our conceptual interpretations of God. Conceptual knowledge about the absolute mystery, such as that which is contained in the traditional "proofs" of God's existence, is the outcome of an a posteriori process of reasoning that objectifies the original experience of the absolute mystery in conceptual terms. We have seen that conceptual reflection is never able to capture an experience totally. This is especially true with the experience of God. Our experiential knowledge of God, since it is always an experience of the absolutely incomprehensible mystery, can never capture or exhaust what can be known about God. Subsequent conceptualizations of that experience are even less able to do so. Our conceptual grasp of our experience of God takes place with varying degrees of clarity and success, and at times we do not even make this transition at all.[9]

We should be cautious, then, about saying that what we experience is "God" or "the absolute mystery," for that presup-

9. K. Rahner, "The Experience of God Today," 149–150; "Observations on the Doctrine of God in Catholic Dogmatics," 127–144; *Encyclopedia of Theology: The Concise* Sacramentum Mundi (New York: Crossroad, 1982) 47–54; and "Experience of Transcendence from the Standpoint of Christian Dogmatics," 177.

poses that we know beforehand what is meant by these terms. It would be better to say that what is meant by the terms is to be understood on the basis of these experiences. The names, images, or concepts that we assign to the object of these experiences are incapable of positively describing the absolute, holy mystery. They simply hint at that which we only faintly perceive hidden within our experiences of our graced transcendence. Our original, basic experiences of God supply whatever content and meaning our conceptual language about God possesses. But we should always remember that there is a permanent and insurmountable difference between our experience of God and our rhetoric about God. The reality of the absolute mystery will always infinitely exceed anything we might be able to say about it. That is not to say that we cannot understand anything about God. It only means that whatever we do accurately understand about God still falls immeasurably short of fathoming the depths of God. If our discourse about God is not going to prove disastrously misleading, it must always be referred back to our fundamentally ineffable experiences of absolute mystery.[10]

Christianity attempts to lead us again and again into the gracious abyss of absolute mystery. The experience of God is the experience of the nearness of the absolute mystery of God, who brings mercy and reconciliation and freely invites us to participate in the divine life. In Christianity, this experience of grace is revealed as victorious in Jesus Christ and permanently present in our history. Therefore, Rahner says that "among the religions which *de facto* exist (considered as historical and social phenomena) it is precisely Christianity which makes real this experience of God in its most radical and purest form, and in Jesus Christ achieves a convincing manifestation of it in history."[11]

This experience of God constitutes the heart of Christianity. But the experience of the absolute mystery lies so deeply hidden within ordinary life and is so difficult to conceptualize, imagine,

10. K. Rahner, "Christianity and the Non-Christian Religions," 115–134; "Church, Churches and Religions," TI 10 (New York: Seabury, 1977) 30–49; and "The One Christ and the Universality of Salvation," 199–224.
11. K. Rahner, "The Experience of God Today," 164.

or articulate that even the most committed of Christians may find themselves virtually oblivious of it. The brilliance of the ever-present darkness of God is so blinding that we need to taught how to see again and again. It is, then, "a task precisely for Christianity itself to point ever anew to this basic experience of God, to induce man to discover it within himself, to accept it and also to avow his allegiance to it in its verbal and historical objectivation; for, in its pure form and as related to Jesus Christ as its seal of authenticity, it is precisely this that we call Christianity."[12]

THE MYSTICISM OF DAILY LIFE

Rahner developed his theology of worship to help those of us who are tempted to dismiss the Church's liturgy as so much archaic ritual that is irrelevant to our search for God. Most of us probably find ourselves thinking this at one time or another; and if we do not, maybe we should. After all, are our liturgical assemblies such powerful encounters with the absolute, holy mystery that we emerge from them radically renewed and fundamentally transformed? Does worshiping together leave us hungering and thirsting to be holy as God is holy? Does our experience of the liturgy arouse honest conversion to the living God, heartfelt communion with our neighbor, and compassionate commitment to the victims of injustice? Those of us who do worship on anything like a regular basis certainly experience some of these things at least occasionally. But unfortunately, the typical experience in our worshiping communities seems to fall far short of these aspirations. For most, the liturgy provides some measure of consolation, at least through its familiarity and routine. But the routine of it all can easily lull us into complacency about God, one another, and the plight of the poor. And when it does, the liturgy seems less and less able to satisfy the deepest desires of our hearts.

Our liturgies provide little help when we feel overwhelmed by the apparent absence of God in our lives and our world. Measured against the intractable suffering of the poor, and the recur-

12. Ibid., 164–165.

ring pain in our own lives, whatever consolation the liturgy provides seems far too meager. We gather together hoping to meet the God who seems so impossible to find in our everyday world. Perhaps we assume that our world is so secular and sinful that God cannot be found there, but only in special sacred places. Perhaps we succumb to the temptation to use worship as an escape from the emptiness and meaninglessness of our daily lives. Perhaps we presume that we should just ignore our suffering and pain, reassuring ourselves that despite it all, life is good and God is with us. Since we cannot seem to find God in our bad experiences, it is easy to imagine that we have to find God in spite of them. But the more pain and suffering we suppress, the more difficult it is to trust that a gracious God is really present. It gets increasingly difficult for our fleeting experiences of God within our worshiping community to balance our persistent experiences of meaninglessness and evil outside it. We may continue to go through the motions of participating in the liturgy. But we may be tempted to abandon it as a pointless ritual and concentrate our search for God elsewhere. Or, even worse, perhaps we are tempted to just abandon the search for God altogether. Does this God that the liturgy describes so poetically really even exist?

Rahner is convinced that the liturgy will become a life-giving encounter with the absolute mystery only if we first discover the experience of God hidden in the midst of our daily lives. If we cannot see God in the ordinary events of life, both the bad and the good, we cannot expect that we will suddenly be able to see God when we gather to worship. Granted, extraordinary events like worship can be much more conducive to revealing the presence of God than many other events in life. Nonetheless, the Church's liturgy is also an ordinary event celebrated by ordinary people like ourselves. Our attentiveness to the presence of God in worship, therefore, directly depends upon our attentiveness to God in daily life. To the extent that we have a heightened awareness of the absolute mystery in all the joys and sufferings of life, we will have little trouble finding God in the liturgical assembly. But to the degree that we are oblivious to that experience of absolute mystery that is an inescapable, secret ingredient of every human experience, we will be equally unresponsive to God in the experience of worship. Before worship can be an explicit experience of God, daily life must be an explicit experience of God. Rahner says to those of us who are tempted to think that the liturgy is useless: "It must be admitted readily and without hesitation to such people that grace, encounter with God, can occur and does actually occur in the ordinary routine of secular life. Prior to any kind of defense of the Church's liturgy, for these people in the first place there must be produced a clear way of access to the depths of their own existence, where God has communicated himself from the very beginning."[13]

Rahner thinks that all of us, not only those who may have difficulty with worship, should try to discover the experience of absolute mystery, which pervades everyday life. It is an experience available to everyone and the very heart of Christianity. But it is also an experience that is easily ignored or overlooked, and so we must "dig it out, so to speak, from under the refuse of the ordinary business of life."[14] Rahner concludes, therefore, that Christians must become "mystics," people who are increasingly attuned to the presence of the absolute mystery of God in their lives.[15]

The heart of the mystical experience is the experience of the absolute mystery of God. That experience can take place with or without the extraordinary phenomena usually associated with mysticism. Mysticism is conventionally identified with unusual psychophysical phenomena such as visions, locutions, ecstasies, dreams, and trances. If these are considered to be the distinguishing characteristics of mysticism, it is clearly a rare event. Within this understanding of mysticism, mystics are a very elite

13. Karl Rahner, "On the Theology of Worship," TI 19 (New York: Crossroad, 1983) 148.

14. K. Rahner, "Experience of the Holy Spirit," 202.

15. Karl Rahner, "Christian Living Formerly and Today," TI 7 (New York: Seabury, 1977) 15. *See also* Harvey Egan, "The Devout Christian of the Future Will . . . Be a 'Mystic.' Mysticism and Karl Rahner's Theology," *Theology and Discovery: Essays in Honor of Karl Rahner, S.J.*, ed. W. J. Kelly (Milwaukee: Marquette University Press, 1980) 139–158.

group, and their experience of God is not something we would expect to share. But Rahner argues that the psychophysical phenomena usually identified with mysticism are secondary gifts that are only sometimes given with the greater gift of the experience of God. The secondary gifts should not be confused with the primary gift. Experience of God is in fact normally offered to us without any of these ancillary gifts.[16] If we distinguish the central mystical experience from the rare marginal phenomena, "then it would be easier to understand that such mystical experiences are certainly not occurrences lying completely outside the experience of an ordinary Christian; that what the mystics talk about is an experience which any Christian (and indeed any human being) can have and can seek, but which is easily overlooked or suppressed. But in any case it is true that mysticism exists and it is not as remote from us as we are at first tempted to assume."[17]

Mysticism, in other words, is not a gift reserved for an elite corps of Christians. Mysticism has to do essentially with our experience of transcendence and our basic experience of God. In this sense, hidden, anonymous mystical experiences are as inescapable as the experience of transcendence.[18] Rahner says, "If we wanted to describe as 'mysticism' this experience of transcendence in which man in the midst of ordinary life is always beyond himself and beyond the particular object with which he is concerned, we might say that mysticism always occurs, concealed and namelessly, in the midst of ordinary life and is the condition of the possibility for the most down-to-earth and most secular experience of ordinary life."[19] We can and should become mystics

16. Karl Rahner, "Mystical Experience and Mystical Theology," TI 17 (New York: Crossroad, 1981) 90–99; and "Ein Brief von P. Karl Rahner," *Der Mensch als Geheimnis: Die Anthropologie Karl Rahners* von Klaus Fischer (Freiburg: Herder, 1974) 400–410. *See also* Harvey Egan, *What Are They Saying About Mysticism?* (New York: Paulist, 1982) 98–108.

17. K. Rahner, "Experience of the Holy Spirit," 193.

18. K. Rahner, "The Experience of God Today," 153; and "Experience of Transcendence from the Standpoint of Catholic Dogmatics," 174–176.

19. K. Rahner, "Experience of the Holy Spirit," 197. *See also* Karl Rahner, "Mysticism," *Encyclopedia of Theology: The Concise Sacramentum Mundi*, 1010–1011.

because we can and should become increasingly aware of this hidden experience of absolute mystery, which is so easily overlooked or suppressed. If worship is ever to become a transforming experience of God, we need to become more and more deeply aware of the experience of the absolute mystery in our daily lives.[20]

But the experience of God is so completely and constantly available in daily life that it is frequently ignored, misinterpreted, or suppressed. "In everyday life this transcendental experience of God in the Holy Spirit remains anonymous, implicit, unthematic, like the widely and diffusely spread light of a sun which we do not directly see, while we turn only to the individual objects visible in this light in our sense-experience."[21] We need, therefore, to be guided into this experience. We need help to notice, understand, and accept our own mystical experiences; we must be provided with a "mystagogy" of the mysticism of ordinary life. Such a process would be designed to help us discover and appropriate the experience of God that is present throughout the course of our daily lives.[22] For those who are confused or frustrated by the quality of our liturgical life, "such a mystagogy is a necessary presupposition for an understanding of the Church's worship. If this understanding is to be awakened, they must be shown that worship is the explicit celebration of the divine depth of their ordinary life, that what clearly appears in it and consequently can be more decisively accepted in freedom is what occurs always and everywhere in the ordinary course of life."[23]

A mystagogical formation is necessary because the experience of God, even more so than any other basic experience, cannot be completely captured and communicated in conceptual categories.

20. Karl Rahner, "Considerations on the Active Role of the Person in the Sacramental Event," TI 14 (New York: Seabury, 1976) 172–173.

21. K. Rahner, "Experience of the Holy Spirit," 199.

22. K. Rahner, "On the Theology of Worship," 148. *See also* Klaus P. Fischer, "Wo der Mensch an das Geheimnis grenzt. Die mystagogische Struktur der Theologie Karl Rahners," ZKTh 98 (1976) 159–170; and J. Bacik, *Apologetics and the Eclipse of Mystery*, 12–19, 39–47.

23. K. Rahner, "On the Theology of Worship," 149.

Something more than information about the experience of God is required, since such information cannot communicate the immediacy of the basic experience.

"The concepts and terms that we use subsequently of this infinity to which we are continually referred do not represent the original form of our experience of the nameless mystery that surrounds the island of our ordinary consciousness, but the small signs and images that we set up and must set up to remind us continually of the original, unthematic experience—silently present and silencing its presence—of the strangeness of the mystery in which we live, despite the clarity of ordinary consciousness, as in a night and in a pathless desert, reminding us of the abyss in which we are unfathomably rooted."[24]

More than education about God, we need direction to God, direction that will guide us in searching out our own experiences of God. We need to be guided toward that absolute mystery, which is "the underlying substrate which is presupposed to and sustains the reality we know."[25] Our preapprehension of this mystery is the condition of possibility for the acts of knowledge and freedom that fulfill our existence. As Rahner says:

"We exist, think and act in freedom only in virtue of the fact that we have already all along transcended that which is specific and particular, that which we can comprehend, in a movement which knows no boundaries. The moment we become aware of ourselves precisely *as* the limited being which in so many and such radical ways we are, we have already overstepped these boundaries. . . . We have experienced ourselves as beings which constantly reach out beyond themselves towards that which cannot be comprehended or circumscribed, that which precisely as having this radical status must be called infinite, that which is sheer mystery. . . . It is present as the abiding mystery."[26]

24. K. Rahner, "Experience of the Holy Spirit," 196.
25. K. Rahner, "The Experience of God Today," 155.
26. Ibid., 155–156.

Mysticism is a matter of searching out this hidden experience of the abiding, absolute mystery of God. While God is always present to us, some events refer us more clearly than others to the incomprehensible mystery that surrounds us. We must be careful, however, not to presume that our "positive" experiences are the ones that will best, or most often, provide us with an explicit experience of God. Sometimes an explicit experience of the absolute mystery is provided by a positive event in daily life. The beauty, joyfulness, or goodness of a particular experience might well be a compelling revelation of the presence of God. For example, experiences in which we witness a majestic sunset, celebrate with a faithful friend, are awed by the immensity of the ocean, are unconditionally loved by a parent, wonder at the splendor of the stars, play with a child, marvel at the grandeur of a mountain range, or delight in the passion of a lover can all be powerful experiences of the absolute mystery. Our desire to be increasingly attentive to the presence of God should lead us to contemplate moments such as these and all the everyday instances of joy, peace, beauty, and goodness we so often take for granted.

But as much as such positive events can be explicit experiences of God, "negative" experiences, times of limitation, sacrifice, pain, and loss, can be even more explicit experiences of the mystery of God. The experience of God is perceived most clearly "where the definable limits of our everyday realities break down and are dissolved, where the decline of these realities is perceived, when lights shining over the tiny island of our ordinary life are extinguished and the question becomes inescapable, whether the night that surrounds us is the void of absurdity and death that engulfs us or the blessed holy night already shining within us is the promise of eternal day."[27]

The experience of God is present every time we exercise our transcendence. But, for Rahner, it manifests itself more clearly in those times in which "the individual, normally lost amid the individual affairs and tasks of his everyday life, is to some extent thrown back upon himself and brought to a position in which he

27. K. Rahner, "Experience of the Holy Spirit," 199–200.

can no longer overlook those factors in his life which he customarily evades."[28] This takes place, for example, when we face loneliness and isolation, when we accept responsibility for our sinfulness, when we are faithful to our commitments at great cost to ourselves, when we freely surrender in self-sacrificing obedience to one another, when we calmly accept sickness and diminishment, when we courageously commit ourselves to justice and peace for all, when we seek reconciliation with our worst enemies, when we sincerely forgive people who break our hearts, and especially when we confront death, our own or that of someone we cherish. Times like these jar us out of our complacency and challenge us to reaffirm our most basic values. They shatter our comfortable presuppositions about ourselves and force us to make fundamental choices about what kind of people we want to be. They compel us to make some of our clearest acts of free self-realization and so offer us some of our clearest experiences of God. More so than any others, these experiences bring us face to face with ourselves and so face to face with the absolute mystery.[29]

Through such experiences we can discover that God is present in every moment, no matter how "negative" it might be. Their common thread is that they are all experiences of limitation. We confront in them, sometimes in extremely painful ways, our personal limits. We are forced to come to terms with the limits of one another, of our relationships, of our families and communities, of our world, and of life itself. In these experiences, we are compelled to recognize the often bitter consequences of our historicity and materiality. But precisely because these are such powerful experiences of limitation, they can be equally powerful experiences of transcendence. We could not experience these limits as limits unless we were also able to go beyond them. When these experiences are particularly painful, we may feel completely overcome by suffering. All we may recognize at such

28. K. Rahner, "The Experience of God Today," 157.
29. K. Rahner, "Experience of the Holy Spirit," 200–203; "The Experience of God Today," 157–159; and "Reflections on the Experience of Grace," 87–88. See also James Bacik's models of mystery in Apologetics and the Eclipse of Mystery, 65–126.

times is loss, deprivation, and defeat. But if we are able to accept these limits as limits, and in that way accept the fact that we are not completely determined by them, we can have a powerful experience of transcendence. To know that we have limits but to perceive that there is something beyond those limits is to experience transcendence. To perceive that there is something beyond our limits and to affirm the good we may glimpse only dimly there is to experience God. And to do this again and again is to gradually discover that God is present in every experience, no matter how negative.

Every "negative" experience, no matter how painful, has a "positive" side to it. There is no event in which we cannot experience God. This does not mean that suffering and evil are actually good things, they are not. The plight of the world's poor, for example, is an intolerable injustice. The fact that we might glimpse the presence of God in their suffering does not give us license to be complacent but should only rekindle our desire to do everything in our power to alleviate their injustices. If God is present with them in their pain, we should be as well. Nor does the fact that we can find God in experiences of evil mean that suffering will not continue to be painful. We continue to experience God in these moments precisely because they continue to be painful reminders of our limitations. And the painful parts of these events are much more likely to dominate our attention than the presence of God is.

All such experiences of pain, suffering, and evil, however, can be explicit experiences of God. This means that there is nothing in life so secular or sinful that we cannot find God in it. It means that we live in a fallen world, which is in fact permeated by grace. The liturgy is not a refuge from a harsh and merciless world. We should never treat it as an escape from the emptiness and meaninglessness of our lives. We do not have to ignore or deny the intractable suffering of the world in order to preserve some semblance of faith in God. We can find God in all the moments of our day, even the ones that seem furthest from God. Granted, we usually have a difficult time seeing the absolute mystery there. But that is often because we do not expect to find God there. It is easy for us to assume that God could not, or would not, be present in such moments. But if we have the courage and patience to look, we may be surprised to find a God we might never have hoped for or imagined.

These examples of positive and negative experiences are but a few of the ways in which we can discern the abiding presence of the absolute, holy mystery in daily life. Such experiences lead us to "that experience which is ultimate and yet present at the same time everywhere in our everyday lives, for in these man is forever occupied with the grains of sand along the shore where he dwells at the edge of the infinite ocean of mystery."[30]

Each moment of our lives is like a grain of sand lying just alongside the ocean of mystery. Every event, no matter how profane or mundane it might seem, is a potential experience of God. The basic material of our experience of God, then, need not be anything that is overtly religious. We do not have to conceptualize or articulate our experiences in religious categories for them to be experiences of God. In fact, the experience of God does not normally take place in religious ways. "In most cases in human life this does not come about expressly in meditation, in experiences of absorption, etc., but on the material of normal life: that is, when responsibility, fidelity, love, etc., are realized absolutely, while even in the very last resort it remains a secondary question whether this activity is accompanied by an explicitly religious interpretation, although (conversely) it is not denied that a religious interpretation of this kind is right and also important as such."[31] The explicitly religious moments of our lives, experiences of the Church's liturgy, for example, are necessary and important symbolic manifestations of the presence of God in all our moments. But they are just that; they are not the only times that God is present. We will only be able to recognize the presence of the absolute mystery in the liturgy if we recognize its abiding presence throughout our lives and our world.

Our liturgical problems will not simply disappear if we are more conscious of our experiences of God in the course of daily

30. K. Rahner, "The Experience of God Today," 159.
31. K. Rahner, "Experience of the Holy Spirit," 207. *See also* "Experience of the Spirit and Existential Commitment," 28.

life. A mystagogy into the mysticism of daily life will not guarantee that our liturgical assemblies will become transparent experiences of the kingdom of God. Worship will always seem somewhat awkward, archaic, and confusing. Communion and communication with the living God are perplexing even for mystics. God is so radically different from us that it will always be difficult to achieve a personal relationship with God.[32] Nonetheless, Rahner thinks that if we were to become mystics, we would develop a much deeper appreciation of worship. If nothing else, the liturgy would not seem to be irrelevant to our search for God. The experience of the absolute mystery of God can then begin to teach us the meaning of adoration, that "total commitment in which man falls into silence, in which the word he addresses to God is merely the prelude to his silence, in which he veils his countenance before the majesty of the ineffable mystery, and in which he is aware that contrary to all appearances today man cannot contend with God."[33]

Above all, the experience of absolute mystery will lead us to realize the utter audacity of addressing God. Then we might begin to realize that such an opportunity to encounter God is a gift of pure grace. To this end, Rahner recommends that we learn from Jesus. "It is no matter for regret, if we find the courage to address God in this way only by keeping our eyes fixed upon Jesus, seeing that even in death he still managed to call this mystery 'Father,' and to surrender himself into his hands even as, in slaying him, it withdrew itself from him and threw him into the most inconceivable state of dereliction from God."[34]

32. K. Rahner, "The Experience of God Today," 162–163.
33. Ibid., 163.
34. Ibid.

Chapter Four

The Liturgy of the World

Worship, like any other human activity, is always an experience of God. Such experience of God is a continual source of wonder and cause for celebration. But this is not because it is anything unusual or uncommon. The experience of God never ceases to be a gift, not because it is only rarely given to us but because it never ceases to be an experience *of God*. At some level of our consciousness, we are always experiencing the absolute mystery, at least implicitly. And at some level of our free acts, we are always accepting or resisting God. Every moment of every day has the potential to become an explicit, mutual experience of God, in which God chooses to become present to us and we choose to become present to God. Such communion and interaction with God may very well take place in obviously religious situations, for example, when we are alone at prayer or together in worship; but it need not. The most joyful and the most tragic, the most extraordinary and the most mundane events of human life can all become experiences of full and active participation in the life of God.

The abiding, gracious presence of the absolute mystery is not something that has just recently been discovered. Our's is certainly not the first generation to experience communion with God. If cooperation with God is an indispensable, secret ingredient of our lives, it is also an essential but generally hidden dynamic of human history. Every moment in human history, no matter how inconsequential or profane it might seem, has the potential to manifest God. Every people in every age somehow experiences the presence of the absolute mystery, even if this happens only in very obscure ways. And every human community is given the opportunity to cooperate with God in creation and redemption. When this interaction with God in history becomes explicit, it is not necessarily grasped in specifically religious ways. Ordinary and ostensibly secular events in the world's history become explicit manifestations of our relationship with God. Our individual experiences of the absolute mystery, then, are small parts of a much bigger process, a process that includes all of human history from beginning to end. Participation in the life and activity of God is an inescapable, secret ingredient of human history.

In other words, the history of the world is a liturgy. By saying this, we are not presuming that we already know what we mean by liturgy. Our goal is not to explain history in terms of liturgy, but liturgy in terms of history. For Rahner, the history of the world is the original liturgy; it gives the primary content and meaning to our concept of liturgy. This perspective grounds the basic methodology of Rahner's theology of worship. Whenever he addresses a particular question about liturgy, worship, sacraments, or prayer, Rahner ultimately refers the topic back to the fundamental experience of the liturgy of the world. He may not always adopt this terminology, in fact the expression "liturgy of the world" appears rather infrequently, but he always adopts this viewpoint. The final answers to any questions about worship are always to be found hidden in the dynamics of the universal self-communication of the mystery of God effecting a response in our freedom. For Rahner, all theology of worship is primarily theology of the liturgy of the world.

THE UNIVERSAL HISTORY OF SALVATION

Rahner sees revelation and salvation taking place throughout the full range of human history. Our transcendental openness to God is universally graced by the offer of God's self-communication. But the holy mystery's gracious self-communication is always mediated to us by the particular categorical realities in and through which we experience our transcendence. Likewise, our free response to God's self-communication is always categorically mediated. We accept or reject salvation through the concrete choices we make in the ordinary, everyday exercise of our freedom. Both God's free self-communication in grace and our free response to God's offer are mediated by specific historical realities. And the converse is also true: At some level, any fully human historical experience mediates the absolute mystery's self-revelation and our affirmation or denial of that offer of salvation.[1]

We do not, then, only interact with God when we are explicitly conscious of our relationship with God. Every genuinely human experience somehow mediates an experience of the holy mystery, at least implicitly. This experience is not simply a passive awareness of God, it is always also an active response to God. Our response may only be an implied affirmation of our previous, fundamental acceptance or denial of God. But even that minimal exercise of our freedom is an essential part of our self-realization in relationship to God. Every human, historical experience, therefore, mediates God's presence to us and our presence to the absolute mystery. The necessary historical mediations of God's saving self-revelation and our response to it take place not only in specifically and explicitly religious events, but everywhere. Perfectly ordinary and ostensibly profane events can and do mediate our relationship with the absolute mystery.

The necessary categorical mediation of our interaction with God is never static. It is a free event, both on our part and on God's, which takes place in time as well as in space, and so it has a history. God's free offer of salvation and our free response unfold in human history. But again, given the universal salvific will of God, this historical mediation of revelation and salvation is not restricted to the history of obviously religious events. Salvation history takes place secretly and anonymously throughout the ordinary history of the world. "Hence the freedom of acceptance or refusal of salvation occurs in all the dimensions of human existence, and it occurs always in an encounter with the

1. *See* Karl Rahner, "History of the World and Salvation-History," TI 5 (New York: Crossroad, 1983) 97–114; *Foundations of Christian Faith: An Introduction to the Idea of Christianity* (New York: Seabury, 1978) 138–175; "Observations on the Concept of Revelation," *Revelation and Tradition*, Karl Rahner and J. Ratzinger (Freiburg: Herder, 1966) 9–25; "Revelation": 1, "Concept of Revelation," B, "Theological Interpretation," *Encyclopedia of Theology: The Concise* Sacramentum Mundi (New York: Crossroad, 1982) 1460–1466; and "The Order of Redemption Within the Order of Creation," *The Christian Commitment: Essays in Pastoral Theology* (New York: Sheed and Ward, 1963).

world and not merely in the confined sector of the sacred or of worship and 'religion' in the narrow sense, it occurs in encounters with one's neighbor, with one's historical task, with the so-called world of everyday life, in and with what we call the history of the individual and of communities. Thus salvation-history takes place right in the midst of ordinary history.''[2]

In the midst of all the ordinary and extraordinary events that fill human history, we receive and respond to the absolute mystery's gracious self-communication. The history of revelation is not restricted to the Jewish and Christian Scriptures but is coextensive with the whole human story. The history of salvation is not restricted to the great moments in the world's religions but is coextensive with the entire human enterprise. History, then, cannot be divided into exclusively secular and sacred tracks. There is no such thing as a purely secular history that develops alongside a purely sacred history. Sacred events are historical events in which our interaction with God becomes more explicit than is normally the case. Secular events, however, always involve a hidden, secret human interaction with the absolute mystery. Our individual and collective sacred histories occur within a larger secular history, which is itself permeated with the effective grace of God. The dialogue between the absolute mystery and humankind continues throughout history. In the actual world in which we live, there is no such thing as purely secular and profane history. If "pure nature" is a concept that is necessary to maintain the gratuity of grace but is not an experienced reality of the actual world in which we live, then the same may be said about the notion of "profane history."

The history of salvation, therefore, is coextensive with the whole history of the human race. It is not identical with that history because the world's history also includes guilt and the rejection of God. We should never minimize the tragic reality of sin in our individual and collective histories. We are culpable of rejecting and resisting God not only in our obviously malicious moments but in countless everyday activities that would appear to be quite harmless. Nonetheless, we should also never allow

2. K. Rahner, "History of the World and Salvation-History," 98–99.

our experiences of sin to overshadow the reality of grace and salvation in human history. Insofar as everything historically tangible in human existence engages our transcendence and freedom, the history of salvation is necessarily coextensive with all history. Wherever human history is lived and suffered in freedom, the histories of both sin and salvation are also taking place. The history of salvation does not take place just where our history is actualized in explicitly religious ways. It encompasses the apparently profane history of our lives and our world.

Salvation history, however, lies inescapably hidden within ordinary history, since the saving or damning nature of historical events is never unambiguously apparent. Ordinary history generally does not give any unequivocal indication of the salvation or damnation taking place within it. The saving or damning characteristics of free decisions remain hidden from ourselves and one another. They do not by themselves become objectively tangible facts, and so our historical journeys are always pilgrimages made in hope and faith. We can never step completely back from our history and definitively determine whether it is a history of salvation or not. The quality of the interaction with God taking place in every event of our individual and collective histories always remains to some extent hidden from us.

A special and explicit history of revelation can, however, be distinguished from the general history of revelation, which is coextensive with world history. The self-revelation of God, which is coextensive with world history, provides us with a nonconceptual awareness of God, which must be interpreted and translated in conceptual terms. This process of interpretation has a history that God guides, and so, is another divine revelation within the context of God's general revelation. When God so directs the interpretation of revelation that it remains permanently valid, then we have what is known as public and official revelation. This explicit history of revelation, embodied in the covenant of Israel and in the life of the Church, takes place within the universal history of revelation. Both the general and the special histories of revelation come to their absolute climax in Jesus Christ. He is the full and unsurpassable event of the historical self-interpretation of God's self-communication to the world.

God distinguishes the explicit history of salvation from general human history by guiding the interpretation of a particular part of the ambiguous history of the world. The distinction between the special and general histories of salvation comes from God. The saving acts of God become present in human history precisely as saving acts of God, and so become the explicit history of salvation, only when the word of God which expresses and interprets them is added.

This interpreting word of God is not present universally in human history but only at special times and places. The explicit history of salvation, therefore, is distinguished from history in general whenever our interaction with God is clearly interpreted by God's word. God's interpreting and revealing word differentiates the special history of salvation from the general history of salvation which is coextensive with all human history. The special history of salvation is the valid self-interpretation of God's self-communication to us and the explicit expression of the universal history of this self-communication. This process takes place especially through the prophets who, the Judeo-Christian tradition believes, were enabled by God to correctly interpret their people's interaction with God. This is expressed in the prophets in such a way that it clearly becomes the reliable interpretation of our interaction with God as well.[3]

This distinguishing of the special history of salvation from history in general has itself a history all its own. It has not been equally intense and manifest in every age. Only the history of the people of Israel was interpreted authoritatively by the word of God in such a way that it was thus distinguished from any other history. The history of the people of Israel became the official and special history of salvation in distinction from the rest of human history. This phase of the history of revelation and salvation began with God's covenant with Abraham, had its center in the Exodus from Egypt and the covenant with the chosen people of Israel under Moses at Sinai, and came to fulfillment in the New Testament period in Christ's death and resurrection and the

3. *See* Karl Rahner, "Prophetism," *Encyclopedia of Theology: The Concise Sacramentum Mundi,* 1286–1289.

new and eternal covenant of God with the whole of humanity, which they constituted.[4]

The New Testament period of the history of salvation extends beyond the resurrection of Christ and Pentecost (taken as one salvific event) to Christ's return. This period is the eschatological time, the time when the history of human freedom is no longer simply open in an endless dialectic between salvation and damnation. In this period, the triumphant self-communication of God has been historically manifested in the incarnate Word of God in such a way that the ultimate ground of the history of salvation is present and active as an element of human history. This is what distinguishes the New Testament period of salvation history from that of the Old Testament. The Church, which professes faith in Jesus Christ, is the ongoing presence of this eschatologically triumphant ultimate ground of salvation history.[5]

In Jesus Christ, God's self-communication and humanity's response reach an absolute and indissoluble unity, and in the self-revelation of Jesus this unity becomes historically present. Saving history is clearly and permanently distinguished from all secular history in the Christ event. Everything that follows from this Christ event, such as the Church, the sacraments, and the Scriptures, also participates in its distinction from profane history. The special history of salvation reaches in Christ its clearest and absolutely permanent distinction from history in general and comes to its unequivocally distinct manifestation within the history of the world, thus bringing general salvation history to its fullest self-realization within the history of the world.

The official history of salvation is, therefore, nothing more or less than the process by which that history of salvation, which pervades our lives and extends throughout our history, becomes explicit and historically tangible through the Word of God.

"What we call Church and what we call the explicit and official history of salvation, and hence also what we call the sacraments,

4. Karl Rahner, "History of Salvation: The Old Testament Period," *Encyclopedia of Theology: The Concise Sacramentum Mundi*, 1512–1516.
5. Karl Rahner, "History of Salvation: The New Testament Period," *Encyclopedia of Theology: The Concise Sacramentum Mundi*, 1516–1518; and "Eschatology," ibid., 434–439.

are only especially prominent, historically manifest and clearly tangible events in a history of salvation which is identical with the life of man as a whole. As the universal and collective history of the salvation of all mankind, this salvation history has entered into its final, eschatological and irreversible phase through Jesus Christ. Through Jesus Christ the drama and the dialogue between God and his world has entered into a phase which already implies God's irreversible triumph, and which also makes this victory in the crucified and risen Jesus Christ historically tangible. The all-encompassing word of God has been proclaimed in such a way that its victory and God's 'yes' can no longer be undone by man's 'no.' "[6]

The explicit history of salvation, especially its fulfillment and highpoint in Jesus Christ, is the clear manifestation of the real character of the world's history. Through the power of the Word of God, the events of our explicit salvation history clearly express that interaction and cooperation with the absolute mystery, which is hidden throughout the breadth of human history. The Christ event is the clearest manifestation of the enduring success of humanity's relationship with God. From the Christian point of view, then, the triumphs of human history are not only our great achievements in philosophy, literature, art, politics, science, technology, and so on. All the little moments in which ordinary, anonymous people quietly surrender themselves into the life of the absolute mystery of God are also extraordinary moments in human history. They are not extraordinary because they happen so rarely but because in these moments human beings reach their highest potential: to become one with God. And the lives of those who do achieve this union with the absolute mystery give, even in their most ordinary moments, unspoken praise to God. To have one's daily life become an act of worship is the greatest human achievement.

THE LITURGY OF THE WORLD

The explicit history of salvation reveals that there is a perpetual interaction between God's gracious self-communication to us and

6. K. Rahner, *Foundations of Christian Faith*, 411–412.

our free self-donation to God lying hidden within all human history. In this sense, the history of the world is liturgy for Rahner.[7]

"The world and its history are the terrible and sublime liturgy, breathing of death and sacrifice, which God celebrates and causes to be celebrated in and through human history in its freedom, this being something which he in turn sustains in grace by his sovereign disposition. In the entire length and breadth of this immense history of birth and death, complete superficiality, folly, inadequacy and hatred (all of which 'crucify') on the one hand, and silent submission, responsibility even to death in dying and in joyfulness, in attaining the heights and plumbing the depths, on the other, the true liturgy of the world is present—present in such a way that the liturgy which the Son has brought to its absolute fullness on his Cross belongs intrinsically to it, emerges from it, i.e. from the ultimate source of the grace of the world, and constitutes the supreme point of *this* liturgy from which all else draws its life, because everything else is always dependent upon the supreme point as upon its goal and at the same time sustained by it."[8]

For Rahner, the original liturgy lies hidden within the history of the world. This secret dynamic of human history is not just *a* liturgy, one of a wide variety of possible types of liturgy. Nor is it liturgy in some metaphorical way. The human community's ongoing communion and cooperation with God in history is *the* liturgy, the primary and original liturgy.

As the most basic and fundamental liturgy, this liturgy of the world provides the original objective content for our notion of liturgy. When we think of liturgy, we should think first and foremost of the liturgy of the world. Worship is not primarily what happens when we gather together to celebrate the Eucharist; it is primarily what happens when we cooperate together with God in history. Liturgy is not originally the praise we give to God when we pray; it is what happens when we freely immerse our-

7. Karl Rahner, "Considerations on the Active Role of the Person in the Sacramental Event," TI 14 (New York: Seabury, 1976) 161–184.
8. Ibid., 169–170.

selves in the abiding, absolute mystery during the great and small moments of life. The liturgy is most basically that pattern of God's reconciling self-communication evoking our thankful self-surrender, which is woven inextricably through our history. Worship is fundamentally the quiet, unobtrusive exchange of self-gifts between the absolute mystery and the human community. Here we find the essential experience of God's free self-communication to us and our free self-donation to God. This liturgy, which takes place throughout the world and human history, is the original liturgy. The liturgy of the Church is one way in which the liturgy of the world is revealed and celebrated.

This does not diminish the importance or necessity of the liturgy of the Church. The liturgy of the world requires the liturgy of the Church in the same way that the general history of revelation and salvation requires the special history of revelation and salvation. The liturgy of the world lies hidden within our history. The self-communication of the absolute mystery is concealed within the ordinary events of our lives. Likewise, our free self-surrender to God is normally an implicit element of our self-gift to one another. The liturgy of the world, therefore, is so frequently disguised by the ordinary events with which it takes place that it can easily be overlooked. So Rahner says: "This liturgy of the world is as it were veiled to the darkened eyes and the dulled heart of man which fails to understand its own true nature. This liturgy, therefore must, if the individual is really to share in the celebration of it in all freedom and self-commitment even to death, be interpreted, 'reflected upon' in its ultimate depths in the celebration of that which we are accustomed to call liturgy in the more usual sense."[9]

If the liturgy of the world is to attract our full and active participation, it must be explicitly celebrated. Our graced interaction with God cannot always remain hidden within the flow of history, or it will be forgotten and ignored. The liturgy of the Church gives dramatic expression to the liturgy of the world. It

9. Ibid., 170. *See also* Karl Rahner, "On the Theology of Worship," TI 19 (New York: Crossroad, 1983) 146.

is not the only way in which our communion with God can be explicitly expressed. But without the liturgy of the Church, we would not be able to grasp fully the height and the depth, the length and breadth, of the liturgy of the world.

Furthermore, there is much in our lives and in human history that is antithetical to the liturgy of the world. We cannot avoid the fact that our individual and collective histories include sin and guilt as well as grace and salvation. Patterns of sin and grace are woven together in our world. Christians believe that the liturgy of the world pervades human history. But to what extent we as individuals are in fact participating in that liturgy and not surrendering to sin is always a question. Christians are confident that when the kingdom of God is finally and fully revealed, the history of the world will be completely transformed in communion with God. But whether we as individuals will join in the celebration of that eschatological liturgy remains undecided. If self-obsession is not to dominate our lives, our self-surrender to God must be explicitly and repeatedly reinforced. If the patterns of sin are not to overshadow the patterns of grace, our communion with God must be strengthened and developed. The liturgy of the Church provides a necessary means of conversion to such deeper participation in the liturgy of the world.

Even though the explicit liturgy of the Church is vitally important, worship is not primarily what happens there. First and foremost, liturgy has to do with the ways we give our lives over to the transforming self-communication of the absolute, holy mystery. Such an exchange of self-gifts between God and humanity takes place wherever human beings experience and embrace their graced transcendence. It takes place, therefore, not only in those moments when we are explicitly aware of our communion with God. It also, and normally, takes place whenever we accept and affirm our "positive" and "negative" experiences of God. The affirmation of our experiences of God does not mean that we consciously acknowledge them as experiences of God. It only requires that we freely allow ourselves to be drawn more deeply into the abiding, absolute mystery, however we experience it. This surrender to mystery can and does occur even in what would appear to be the most dreary and mundane moments of life. Worship, then, is not restricted to certain periods or places in the world's history. The entire length and breadth of human history is the setting for our original experience of liturgy. The apparently religious events in history do not begin to tell the whole story of our communion with God. Those events are but the echoes of a much richer liturgy, which goes on throughout human history.

Our greatest potential as human beings is our ability to celebrate the liturgy of the world with God. Our greatest achievement is that we have in fact responded to the invitation to do so. The explicit history of salvation suggests that this is something that humanity has done not just occasionally but again and again. This has usually not been obvious to anyone at the time or even later. The celebration of the liturgy of the world can be so quiet, anonymous, and implicit that it goes completely unnoticed. But it is precisely the fact that our celebration of the liturgy of the world does become such an ordinary, everyday event that makes it such an extraordinary achievement. We have difficulty recognizing the liturgy of the world, not because it occurs so rarely but because it occurs so often. The most remarkable achievement of human history is that our lives have become so intimately intertwined with the life of God that we do not even notice. We have become so accustomed to our immersion in the abiding presence of absolute mystery that we do not even realize that we are taking it for granted.

This is not to say that we should be oblivious of our relationship with God. Sometimes we need to deliberately choose to surrender ourselves into the abyss of mystery or consciously attend to the ever-gracious God. But it is certainly not necessary that we always be conscious of our communion with God. As we have already seen, we are normally unaware of the ordinary, everyday ways our lives render praise to God. Nor is it always even desirable that we become more conscious of our self-surrender to God. The point of our deliberately choosing to give ourselves over to the absolute mystery is that our whole lives become a perpetual act of self-giving. The exercise of our freedom is an exercise in self-realization: We become the choices we make. The more deeply we have chosen to affirm God, the less consciously we need to do so. The goal of consciously deciding to give praise to God is that we become the praise of God.

We should attend to our experience of God, but an explicit, conceptual awareness of our experience of God always removes us at least one step from that experience. Being aware of the fact that we are worshiping God is not the same as worshiping God. When we are conscious of our self-surrender to God, our attention is at least partly on ourselves. We should desire to become mystics and so to be more deeply aware of the abiding presence of God. But that does not necessarily mean that we should always try to be more deeply aware of our relationship with God. The danger in doing so is that we can just become more centered on ourselves. Total self-surrender to the absolute mystery means surrendering our self-attentiveness. Our goal is the beatific vision, which promises complete consciousness of God and not complete consciousness of our relationship with God. We should not be disturbed, therefore, if we have difficulty bringing the liturgy of the world into focus. The fact that we cannot always see how our daily lives are a communion with God does not, of course, necessarily mean that such communion is taking place. But it can be a positive sign that we are appropriately unselfconscious about our relationship with God.

Our difficulty in seeing how pervasive the liturgy of the world really is in human history has everything to do with the vast amount of evil we witness there. The dominant themes of human history often appear to be oppression, violence, and injustice. We have learned to take suffering, terror, misery, and agony for granted in life. The great tragedy of human history is that we deliberately inflict so much of this evil on one another. We seem to be much more accomplished at committing the most unimaginable atrocities than at worshipfully surrendering our lives to God in service of one another.

The dark moments in human history may seem to overshadow all else and eclipse any hope that our history is actually the original act of worship. But even in many of those dark moments, human beings have joined in the liturgy of the world. God is praised whenever we embrace our graced transcendence. As we have already seen, our painful experiences of limitation can be

97

our most powerful experiences of transcendence. The liturgy of the world is celebrated not only by those who rejoice in the beauty of life but also by those who persevere in all its ugliness. In fact, the trusting self-surrender of those who are broken-hearted achieves the deepest communion in the life of God because it requires the greatest act of faith. The worship they give by bearing their suffering is the most profound witness to the gracious presence of the absolute mystery. They do what we would never imagine could be humanly possible and so give eloquent testimony to the transforming power of God. That does not make their misery any less painful, nor does it justify the evils they are forced to endure. It does mean, though, that even our darkest moments can be taken up into the liturgy of the world. Human history is liturgy not despite its darkness but even in its darkness. Whenever we find ourselves somehow affirming the goodness of life in the midst of the most petty or appalling evils, we are participating in the liturgy of the world. When we reflect on our individual and collective histories, therefore, we should not overlook signs of the original liturgy that are to be found there, even in our darkest moments.

Rahner sees the entire universe drawn up into this liturgy of the world. When he says that the world and its history are a liturgy, he means that the material world itself takes part in this graced exchange with the absolute mystery. It is not only the human community that participates in the life of God but the whole cosmos as well. The setting for our original experience of worship is not just human history but the length and breadth of the universe's history. In the next chapter we shall see how the material world transcends itself and becomes spirit in us. The universe becomes present to itself and present to the ground of its existence in the human community. The whole cosmos is taken up and transformed in our history. Through us, the universe receives the divine self-communication and gratefully surrenders itself back to the absolute mystery. The universe, then, does not simply provide a stage for the liturgy of the world; it actively participates in it through us. The liturgy of the world is not only the greatest achievement of human history, it is also the highpoint and fulfillment of cosmic history.

The original, cosmic liturgy takes place in and through our free history, and so that liturgy is fundamentally a human achievement. The self-communication of God is directed toward our freedom, a real freedom made possible by God. God sustains our freedom in such a way that we are genuinely responsible for accepting or rejecting the mystery of grace. We make this choice in and through making the concrete, ordinary choices of our lives. While the liturgy of the world is radically caused and sustained by God, it is nonetheless something we accomplish. We are not called to be passive spectators at the liturgy of the world; it cannot take place unless we freely enter into it. It is a dialogue that God always encourages but whose success depends upon our full and active participation. God invites us to celebrate the original liturgy with him and so makes the actual celebration of that liturgy contingent upon us. If the daily exercise of our freedom constitutes a fundamental affirmation of our experience of God, then we are celebrating the cosmic liturgy whether we are conscious of it or not.

Nonetheless, the liturgy of the world, and therefore all true worship, is first and foremost something that God celebrates. It takes place at the absolutely free and gracious initiative of God. We are invited to respond to that initiative but even our free response is made possible and effected by the grace of God. The gift of freedom empowers us to respond to God in such a way that we really can accept or deny God. Either way, the exercise of our freedom acknowledges our absolute dependence upon God's grace. The liturgy of the world is primarily caused and celebrated by God. Worship is not an activity that we initiate or sustain. It is at heart something that God brings about in us and with which we cooperate. While the liturgy of the world is our greatest human achievement, it is also our greatest gift. The fact that this gift has been lavished upon us does not make it any less of a gift.

WORSHIP AND THE LITURGY OF THE WORLD

Rahner's understanding of the liturgy of the world means that all of human life can implicitly be an act of worship. This is, of course, not something that is usually apparent to us. Normally we are only conscious of our communion with God when we explicitly ritualize it in our liturgical gatherings. Since we mistakenly identify our relationship with God exclusively with those events in which we are clearly and distinctly aware of the abiding presence of absolute mystery, we are inclined to think that this relationship is a rather limited part of our lives. It is easy to think that we have a variety of relationships, for example, with family, friends, neighbors, and colleagues, and that we also have a relationship with God. Likewise, since we arbitrarily reduce liturgy to those times in which we intentionally offer praise and thanksgiving to God, we may see worship as just one of our many activities. We know that we have to do and choose to do all sorts of things: work, attend to our families, take care of the routine business of daily life. Participating in worship appears to be just one more thing to fit into our schedules.

The problem only worsens if we take Rahner's theology to mean not only that life can be an act of worship but that much of our daily lives is in fact a participation in the cosmic liturgy. Rahner suggests that our lives are probably much more deeply intertwined with the absolute mystery than we could ever hope for or imagine. We should at least consider the possibility that we have become so accustomed to the ordinary ways we experience and accept the self-communication of God that it is almost impossible for us to notice them. This synergy, which, hopefully, we discover to be the underlying dynamic of our lives, is the original and basic liturgy. But the more attuned we become to our own active participation in the ordinary wonders of the liturgy of life, the less important the liturgy of the Church may appear. If our lives are already becoming a liturgy, why do we need organized worship?

As we have already seen, we do not have a relationship with God in addition to other relationships. We experience God and relate to God in and through all our relationships. Our relationship with God is inseparable from every relationship we have. We experience God most completely by experiencing ourselves and other people, and whenever we experience ourselves or other people, we also experience God. The love of God is radically united to the love of self and the love of neighbor.

In the same way, worship is not primarily an extra activity, something we need to do in addition to all our other activities. Worship can and should be the basic meaning of everything we do. Any human activity is an implicit act of worship to the extent that we experience and accept the gracious self-communication of God in it. Whenever we accept and affirm the self-communication of God, no matter how mundanely or ambiguously we may experience it, we participate in the liturgy of the world. Worship, then, is not fundamentally something we need to make extra time for in our daily schedules. We should, on the contrary, allow all the activities we are already involved in to be transformed into implicit acts of worship.

This does not mean that the ordinary activities of our lives will become any less ordinary. Nor does it mean that when we work, attend to our families, or take care of the routine business of daily life, we should necessarily be more consciously focused on our interaction with God. It is more important that our communion with God become deeper than that it become clearer. Our gratitude to God is no less real for being implicit and unreflective. In fact, we give glory and praise to God most fundamentally by routinely living in a way that quietly affirms the original goodness to be found in every moment of life, no matter how ordinary. The liturgical renewal that is most urgently needed, therefore, is not the renewal of the liturgy of the Church. It is the renewal that takes place when our daily lives become an implicit and unself-conscious affirmation of God.

Nevertheless, the fact that our daily lives are becoming a liturgy does not in any way diminish the importance of organized, ritualized worship. It means that when we participate in the Church's liturgy, we are not doing something basically different from other activities but explicitly focusing on the deepest meaning of those activities. The liturgy of the Church is the explicit manifestation of the implicit liturgy of our lives. It is not simply identical with that liturgy of the world, but it is so derived from it and deeply united with it that it really expresses the cosmic liturgy and makes it present to us.

In other words, explicit forms of worship are real symbols of the liturgy of the world. They are distinct from that original synergy of our world, but because they are expressions of it, they make the liturgy of the world really present to us. The liturgy of the world is the original experience of God's self-communication and our free acceptance of that grace. The various ritual forms of worship are symbolic manifestations of this liturgy of the world. The relationship between explicit acts of worship and the liturgy of the world is the same as that between a real symbol and the reality it symbolizes.

A real symbol is distinct from the reality it symbolizes, but because it is derived from and united with that reality, it expresses the reality in such a way that it is made really present. There is a fundamental unity-in-difference between a real symbol and the reality it symbolizes. As we have seen, perhaps our best example of this is the relationship between ourselves and our bodies. In the following chapters we will see how the liturgy of the Church, by virtue of its relationship to the risen Christ, is derived from and united with the liturgy of the world. The cosmic liturgy, therefore, is really expressed and made present in the Church's liturgy. The full reality of the liturgy of the world, God's genuine self-communication and our free response, is manifested in our liturgical celebrations. The necessity and value of the liturgy of the Church comes from the unity-in-difference between it and the liturgy of the world.

On the one hand, this unity-in-difference means that we must not confuse the liturgy of the Church and the liturgy of the world; they are distinct from one another. The liturgy of the world is the basic, primordial liturgy. The liturgy of the Church is a complete and profound manifestation of the original liturgy, but it is not the original liturgy itself. Too much of traditional liturgical theology and spirituality has, however, failed to make this distinction. In fact, the liturgy of the Church has often been seen not only as the original liturgy but as the only liturgy. Granted, Eastern Christianity sees the Church's liturgy as a manifestation of the heavenly liturgy and Western Christianity sees the sacrifice of the Mass as a representation of the sacrifice of the cross. But neither of these approaches describes the liturgy of the Church in relationship to that primordial liturgy, which includes cosmic history, salvation history, the Christ event, the eschatological reality of the Church, and the daily life of the Christian. At least, the Eastern Christian approach assumes that the heavenly liturgy is the original and ongoing liturgy. But until the advent of mystery theology in the twentieth century, the Western approach generally assumed that the sacrifice of Christ, while it may be the primordial liturgical act, lies in the past. This has everything to do, of course, with the lack of attention paid to the resurrection in the Western tradition, a point to which we will return in the next chapter.

Especially in the West, then, there is a tendency to confuse the liturgy of the Church with the original liturgy by treating the Church's worship as the only liturgy. Consequently, the Church's liturgy is isolated from, rather than distinguished from, the rest of reality. By this we mean that the traditional Western approach is unable to discern the characteristic features of the worship life of the Church in light of a deeper unity between that worship and the rest of reality. On the contrary, the Western tradition sees the liturgy of the Church as *sui generis*. It cannot grasp the unity-in-difference between the Church's liturgy and creation, salvation history, Christ, the Church, and daily life, because it does not see these realities as the more original liturgy. Liturgical theology and spirituality are left to construct their theories about how such an isolated liturgy brings grace into a fallen world. In the process, they create artificial links between the liturgy and the Church, Christ, and salvation history.

The value of the liturgy of the Church lies in the fact that it is not the original liturgy. Because it is not, it allows us to step outside the liturgy of the world. Without ever leaving the cosmic liturgy behind, it allows us to turn around and see that liturgy which is normally so hidden from us. It gives us the opportunity to reflect on and rehearse for the liturgy of the world. But ritualized worship can only do this to the extent that it is distinguished from the liturgy of the world. If it is confused with the original liturgy, if it is seen as the one and only liturgy, it is incapable of doing so.

On the other hand, the unity-in-difference between a real symbol and what it symbolizes means that we should not separate the liturgy of the Church from the liturgy of the world; they complete each other. If the liturgy of the world never received the explicit manifestation it does in the liturgy of the Church, it would remain an entirely secret ingredient of our history. The liturgy of the world will engage us as fully conscious and free persons only if it is given explicit expression in the Church's worship. And if the liturgy of the Church were not the manifestation of a liturgy that already successfully pervades our lives, it would not have the power to transform us. The Church's worship radically renews us by profoundly expressing that communion with God in which our lives are already rooted. Formal experiences of worship are not occasions in which salvation and grace are made available to a profane world, but manifestations of the holiness of our lives and our world.

"When we say that we celebrate the death of the Lord until he returns, we are saying that we are giving space and time explicitly in our own life to the culmination of the history of the world liturgy which is present in the cross of Jesus. . . . Consequently what happens in worship of this kind is not something that does not occur or has not permanently occurred elsewhere in the world, but something that occurs always and everywhere or has occurred for all time and for everywhere in the world, and is explicitly celebrated, stated, and appropriated."[10]

The Church's worship, then, manifests the holiness of the "secular" dimension of our lives and of our world. The Church's liturgy is not a series of discrete events in which grace comes to a world normally deprived of it. It is, rather, the ritual and symbolic manifestation of the grace that permeates the world. Our liturgies are "a sign of the fact that this entire world belongs to God, a sign precisely of the fact that God is adored, experienced and accepted everywhere as he who, through his 'grace,' has himself set all things free to attain to himself, a sign that this adoration of him takes place not in Jerusalem alone but everywhere in spirit and in truth."[11]

10. K. Rahner, "On the Theology of Worship," 147.
11. K. Rahner, "Considerations on the Active Role of the Person in the Sacramental Event," 169.

Our liturgical assemblies always take place within a graced and redeemed world. It is precisely because they do occur in such a world, because they are a symbol of this liturgy of the world, that they are an event of grace for us. Worship events express the limitlessness of God's grace and thus make that grace available for us. Explicit forms of worship are necessary and valuable precisely because they give expression to the graced realities underlying our lives. The conventional model of the relationship between grace and the world sees the value of liturgy and worship in the fact that these events provide something not otherwise available. For Rahner, the beauty of true worship is that it shows just how graced our lives already are.

"This ecclesial worship is important and significant, not because something happens in it that does not happen elsewhere, but because there is present and explicit in it that which makes the world important, since it is everywhere blessed by grace, by faith, hope and love, and in it there occurred the cross of Christ, which is the culmination of its engraced history and the culmination of the historical explicitness of this history of grace. To anyone who has (or might have had) absolutely no experience in his own life of the history of grace of the world, no experience of the cosmic liturgy, the Church's liturgy could only seem like a strange ritualism, as strange as the sacrificial action of a Vedic priest who feeds the gods and thinks that by his action he is keeping the world on its tracks."[12]

Since worship is the symbolic manifestation of the liturgy of the world, we can only appreciate the full significance of our liturgical practices to the extent that we appreciate the abiding presence of the absolute mystery in our lives. Those who would actively participate in worship "must be shown that worship is the explicit celebration of the divine depth of their ordinary life, that what clearly appears in it and consequently can be more decisively accepted in freedom is what occurs always and everywhere in the ordinary course of life."[13]

12. K. Rahner, "On the Theology of Worship," 147.
13. Ibid., 149.

Chapter Five

Christ and the Liturgy of the World

For Rahner, Jesus Christ is the highpoint and fulfillment of the liturgy of the world. In Christ, the divine-human dialogue, which takes place silently throughout history, finds its absolute and definitive expression. The crucified and risen Lord is the complete and irreversible manifestation of God's self-communication and humanity's self-surrender. That total communion in absolute mystery, which is the universe's highest potential and God's deepest desire, is finally and irrevocably realized in Christ. Since Christ, the cosmic liturgy unfolds in anticipation of that day when the splendor it has already achieved in Christ will be fully revealed. The glorified Christ is, then, the summit and source of the liturgy of the world. No matter what form it takes, worship has an inner dynamism that orients it to Christ. In Christ we find the true meaning of all liturgy, both the liturgy of the world and our explicit forms of worship. It is all revealed in him as a participation in the eschatologically victorious self-communication of God.[1]

1. For a general view of Rahner's Christology, *see* Karl Rahner, "Current Problems in Christology," TI 1 (Baltimore: Helicon, 1961) 149–200; " 'I Believe in Jesus Christ,' Interpreting an Article of Faith," TI 9 (New York: Seabury, 1977) 165–168; "The Two Basic Types of Christology," TI 13 (New York: Crossroad, 1983) 213–223; "Christology Today?" TI 17 (New York: Crossroad, 1981) 24–38; "What Does It Mean Today to Believe in Jesus Christ?" TI 18 (New York: Crossroad, 1983) 143–156; and "The Position of Christology in the Church Between Exegesis and Dogmatics," (New York: Crossroad, 1982) 185–214. *See also* Brian McDermott, "Roman Catholic Christology: Two Recurring Themes," TS 41 (1980) 339–367; Tyron Inbody, "Rahner's Christology: A Critical Assessment," *St. Luke's Journal of Theology* 25 (1982) 294–310; Friedemann Greiner, "Die Menschlichkeit der Offenbarung: Die tranzendentale Grundlegung der Theologie bei K. Rahner im Lichte seiner Christologie," ZKTh 100 (1978) 596–619; Seely Beggiani, "A Case for Logocentric Theology," TS 32 (1971) 371–406; John F. Haught,

One of the ways we can understand how Rahner sees Jesus Christ as the highpoint and fulfillment of the liturgy of the world is to examine his notion of Christ as the absolute Savior. With this approach Rahner situates Christ within a perspective that opens out onto the entire universe and all of human history, for Christ fulfills not only our self-transcendence but the self-transcendence of the entire material cosmos as well.[2]

We must begin with the relationship between matter and spirit. Matter and spirit are not the disparate realities they are often thought to be. We should neither minimize nor deny their genuine diversity nor reduce them to one another. But it makes sense both philosophically and theologically to say that matter and spirit are basically related to one another and that they are

"What is Logocentric Theology?" TS 33 (1972) 120–132; and Karl-Heinz Ohlig, "Impulse zu einer 'Christologie von unten' bei Karl Rahner," *Wagnis Theologie*, hrsg. H. Vorgrimler (Freiburg: Herder, 1979) 259–273.

2. The primary sources for the following are Karl Rahner, "Christology Within an Evolutionary View of the World," TI 5 (New York: Crossroad, 1983) 157–192; *Foundations of Christian Faith: An Introduction to the Idea of Christianity* (New York: Seabury, 1978) 178–212; *Hominisation: The Evolutionary Origin of Man as a Theological Problem* (Freiburg: Herder, 1965); "The Unity of Spirit and Matter in the Christian Understanding of Faith," TI 6 (New York: Crossroad, 1982) 153–177; "Evolution": 2, "Theological," A, "Evolution," B, "Hominisation," *Encyclopedia of Theology: The Concise Sacramentum Mundi* (New York: Crossroad, 1982) 478–488; and "Natural Science and Reasonable Faith," TI 21 (New York: Crossroad, 1988) 16–55. Related material can be found in Karl Rahner, "The One Mediator and the Many Mediations," TI 9 (New York: Seabury, 1977) 169–184; "The Eternal Significance of the Humanity of Jesus for Our Relationship with God," TI 3 (New York: Crossroad, 1982) 35–46; "Jesus Christ in the Non-Christian Religions," TI 17 (New York: Crossroad, 1981) 39–50; "Christology in the Setting of Modern Man's Understanding of Himself and His World," TI 11 (New York: Crossroad, 1982) 215–229; and "The Secret of Life," TI 6 (New York: Crossroad, 1982) 141–152. The useful secondary literature on this topic includes Denise L. Carmody and John T. Carmody, "Christology in Karl Rahner's Evolutionary World View," *Religion in Life* 49 (1980) 195–210; Joseph Donceel, "Causality and Evolution: A Survey of Some Neo-Scholastic Theories," *New Scholasticism* 39 (1965) 295–315; and Heinrick Falk, "Can Spirit Come from Matter?" *International Philosophical Quarterly* 7 (1967) 541–555.

united. Moreover, this unity of matter and spirit has a history, a history in which a basic dynamism of matter to develop into spirit is revealed. This unity of matter and spirit is attributed by Christian theology to their origin, their history, and their final end.[3]

Christians believe that everything, both material and spiritual, has been created by the one God. This means not only that everything comes from the same cause, but also that in coming from that cause, everything has a basic unity. Therefore, matter and spirit are not realities that simply exist alongside each other while being quite separate and unrelated. Matter and everything meant by it has its origin in the same ultimate ground from which created spirit arises. Matter and spirit are united, then, by virtue of their common origin.

Furthermore, the material world is not a kind of neutral stage on which the history of spiritual persons is enacted. Such a view would mean that the material world would remain untouched by spiritual events and that the history of the material world would only accidentally be the scene of the history of spirit. As far as the history of our relationship with God is concerned, we are always considered by Christianity to be bodily, material, and social beings who have a relationship to God in the material dimension of our existence. Our history is always also the history of the material world and vice versa. Matter and spirit are united, therefore, by virtue of their common history.

Christianity also knows of a unity of matter and spirit in their final end. Matter does not belong to a merely provisional period of the history of spirit, a period that must in the end be definitely surpassed. Nor is the perfection of the world as a whole something that can be planned and achieved by the world itself, a final point that would be a factor in history itself. It is, rather, the consummation of this history. It is the fulfillment of a world constituted by both matter and spirit. The final end of all crea-

3. K. Rahner, ''The Unity of Spirit and Matter in the Christian Understanding of Faith,'' 153–177; ''Christology Within an Evolutionary View of the World,'' 161–168; *Hominisation*, 45–93; and *Foundations of Christian Faith*, 178–203.

tion is not the salvation of isolated individuals but rather the kingdom of God, the new heaven and the new earth. The history of matter and the history of spirit find their goal in one and the same point. By moving toward the same goal they have a genuine unity with one another. Since matter and spirit have this unity (but not uniformity), which in Christian teaching appears in their origin, history, and final end, Rahner says, "A Christian theology and philosophy deems it self-evident that spirit and matter have more things in common (to put it this way) than things dividing them."[4]

This unity of matter and spirit is most clearly apparent in the unity within each of us. Each of us is a unity of matter and spirit, which is prior to the diversity of these elements within ourselves. The fact that matter and spirit are mutually related in us is, for instance, evident in the belief that our final consummation will include our whole selves (and the cosmos) and not simply the survival of our spirits. Another example of how this unity of matter and spirit is maintained by Christianity is the concept that the spiritual soul is the form of the body. This ultimately means that every reality in us, including every material reality, is the reality and expression of our spirit. We are not contradictory or provisional composites of matter and spirit. Matter and spirit are two interrelated elements of ourselves, elements that are inseparable without being reducible to one another.[5]

This condition of mutual relatedness between matter and spirit is not simply a static condition. It has a history; it endures in time. With this history in mind, the intrinsic relationship of matter and spirit consists in the fact that matter develops in the direction of spirit; it becomes spirit. Spirit cannot simply be regarded as the immanent product of material development and evolution, since it must originate from a new creative initiative of God. This is indisputable if we hold that the world as a whole

4. K. Rahner, "Christology Within an Evolutionary View of the World," 161.
5. K. Rahner, "The Unity of Spirit and Matter in the Christian Understanding of Faith," 166–171; and "Christology Within an Evolutionary View of the World," 161–163.

stems from the initiative of God. The human spirit came into being only at a very late point in time and presumably also at a very limited point in space within the history of the material world. Nonetheless, the history of the material world and the history of spirit form one history. Spirit is the result of the history of matter. When matter arrived at a certain point in its history, it surpassed itself and became spirit.[6]

The notion of "becoming" here cannot be thought of simply as a "becoming other," in which something becomes different but does not itself become something more. Real becoming must be thought of as "becoming more," as the attainment of something genuinely new. This "more" is not simply something added on to what was there before. It must be something that is both brought about by, and an active surpassing of, what was existing before. In other words, "becoming" must be understood as active self-transcendence.[7]

Such active self-transcendence is an event that must take place by the power of the absolute fullness of being, God. But this active self-transcendence cannot be something that is received passively from God. The absolute being must be so interior to the finite being that is engaged in becoming more that it is the finite being itself that is really empowered to actively achieve transcendence. Otherwise, this would not be the self-transcendence of the finite being. Nonetheless, this power of active self-transcendence must still take place by the power of absolute being and not finite being. The power of self-transcendence must be thought of as distinct from the finite being, because the power of absolute being cannot be a constitutive principle of the essence of a finite being. Self-transcendence takes place through the power of absolute being, which is intrinsic to the finite being yet not part of its essence. Active self-transcendence includes transcendence into what is substantially new, that is, transcendence

6. K. Rahner, "Christology Within an Evolutionary View of the World," 163–164; "The Unity of Spirit and Matter in the Christian Understanding of Faith," 171–174; and *Hominisation*, 62–93.

7. K. Rahner, "The Unity of Spirit and Matter in the Christian Understanding of Faith," 174; "Christology Within an Evolutionary View of the World," 164–165; and *Foundations of Christian Faith*, 183–187.

to a higher nature. Such essential self-transcendence also occurs through the power of absolute being, which is within the creature yet not proper to its essence.[8]

If the preceding is true, and if the world is one and thus has one history, then we can say that matter can and has evolved in the direction of spirit in a movement of essential self-transcendence. This is not to deny the fact that matter and spirit are really distinct. But such a distinction does not exclude the possibility of matter developing toward spirit if there really is a form of active self-transcendence that includes essential development. Matter prepares the way for spirit and develops toward it, moving slowly toward the boundary line, which it then crosses in its actual self-transcendence. The point at which matter becomes spirit is reached in us. We are the self-transcendence of matter.[9]

The fact that we are the self-transcendence of matter means that the history of the material world is united with and fulfilled in our history. The history of the material world develops toward us and continues in us as our history. It is conserved and surpasses itself in us and will reach its fulfillment in and with our freely enacted history. The fulfillment of our history is, of course, hidden in the absolute mystery of God and so is something completely beyond the scope of our natural powers. Yet Christians believe that our history has been graced by the self-communication of that mystery and has become a history of salvation. Therefore, the whole cosmos will find its fulfillment and consummation in and through our history.[10]

Human beings have, therefore, an extraordinarily important place in the material cosmos. Matter transcends itself in us and

8. K. Rahner, "Christology Within an Evolutionary View of the World," 165; "The Unity of Spirit and Matter in the Christian Understanding of Faith," 174-177; and *Hominisation*, 87-93.

9. K. Rahner, "The Unity of Spirit and Matter in the Christian Understanding of Faith," 177; and "Christology Within an Evolutionary View of the World," 161-168.

10. K. Rahner, "Christology Within an Evolutionary View of the World," 168; *Foundations of Christian Faith*, 187-188; and *Encyclopedia of Theology: The Concise* Sacramentum Mundi, 478-488.

becomes spirit, which means that it becomes both present to it-self and oriented toward the absolute mystery of God. The material world becomes present to itself in us and is no longer related to the absolute mystery of God merely as the ground of its existence. The universe finds in us the possibility of an explicit and direct relationship to God. We are of the utmost importance to the cosmos because it is in us that the entire universe finds the possibility of an immediate relationship to the absolute mystery of God.

This recapitulation of the cosmos is something that is intended to happen and can happen in everyone. The self-presence of the cosmos and consciousness of its orientation to its absolute and infinite foundation takes place in the activity of the human race in general and in each one of us in particular. Through our bodies each of us is always part of the cosmos. We communicate through our bodies with the whole universe in such a way that through this corporeality, the universe achieves its self-presence and its consciousness of its orientation toward God.[11]

Although it is not always apparent to us, this process is moving in a specific direction. The self-transcendence of the material world is moving toward a final consummation in which the cosmos is not only related to its ultimate ground as a distant and aloof horizon, but actually receives the self-communication of the mystery of God in grace and, ultimately, in the beatific vision. In other words, the whole universe is oriented toward a fulfillment that will be achieved when we receive the self-communication of God. The self-transcendence of the cosmos from matter into spirit is a dynamic that is oriented toward receiving the self-communication of God. This fulfillment of the universe can take place only in us, since we are the point at which the universe becomes consciously directed toward God. The development of the cosmos is moving through us and in our history in the direction of an ever-greater intimacy with the absolute mystery of God. The goal of the universe, then, is God's self-communication to it and its free acceptance of that gift. The dy-

11. K. Rahner, ''Christology Within an Evolutionary View of the World,'' 169–171; and *Foundations of Christian Faith*, 188–190.

namism that God has implanted in the very heart of the world's becoming moves toward this self-communication and its acceptance by the world through us.[12]

This self-communication of God is directed to our freedom and interrelatedness. It is necessarily directed to our freedom because it is meant to be actively accepted, not just passively received. Likewise, it is addressed to us in our one common history. The history of the world's self-transcending in us is always a history of our interrelatedness. If the world's becoming conscious of itself did not imply such an interrelatedness among us, it would divide rather than unify. The self-communication of God, therefore, is addressed to our free history and can only take place through our free acceptance in a common history. God's self-communication is, properly speaking, a historical event. The event of God's self-communication takes place historically at definite points in space and time, and from there it is addressed to all people in their freedom. This fulfillment of the dynamism of the universe must have a permanent beginning and must be manifestly irrevocable if it is truly to be the fulfillment of the universe's self-transcendence.[13]

Rahner calls that historical person, in whom this divine self-communication has its beginning, its irrevocable manifestation, and its guarantee, the absolute Savior. This does not mean that this self-communication begins in time only with the absolute Savior. God's self-communication does begin before the coming of the Savior and is in fact coextensive with our whole history. But the self-communication of God to us, even when it takes place during the time before the coming of the Savior, is directed toward and based on this Savior and in this sense begins in him.

The absolute Savior is the one in whom God's self-communication is irrevocably present, is clearly recognized as irrevocable, and so reaches its climax. This divine self-communication is free on God's part. Likewise it must be freely accepted on the part of human history. Therefore, it is possible

12. K. Rahner, *Foundations of Christian Faith*, 190–191; and "Christology Within an Evolutionary View of the World," 171–173.

13. K. Rahner, "Christology Within an Evolutionary View of the World," 173–174; and *Foundations of Christian Faith*, 191–193.

for there to be a historical event in which this free self-communication and its free acceptance become irrevocable and irreversible. The irreversibility of what is achieved in the absolute Savior refers both to God's self-communication and to its acceptance in our history.[14] So Rahner says:

"This whole movement of this history of God's self-communication lives by virtue of its moving towards its goal or its climax in the event by which it becomes irreversible, and hence precisely by virtue of what we are calling the absolute savior. Therefore this savior, who constitutes the climax of God's self-communication to the world, must be at the same time *both* the absolute promise of God to spiritual creatures as a whole *and* the acceptance of this self-communication by the savior, for otherwise of course history could not have reached its irreversible phase. Only then is there an absolutely irrevocable self-communication on both sides, and only then is it present in the world in a historical and communicable way."[15]

Jesus Christ is this irrevocable manifestation of God's self-communication and its acceptance, and so he is the absolute Savior. Although Jesus Christ is a unique event and even the highest conceivable event, he is nevertheless an intrinsic moment within the whole process by which the self-communication of God is offered to the entire world. If this total event of the bestowal of grace on all people is to find its fulfillment, it must become historically tangible. This fulfillment cannot be acosmic or metahistorical; it must take place in such a way that this event emanates from one point in time and space. It must be a reality in which God's self-communication is shown to be not a mere conditional and revocable offer but unconditional and accepted by humanity. This is precisely what happens in Christ. In Christ, God brings about our self-transcendence into the absolute mystery through God's own self-communication to all people in such a way that it is irrevocable.[16]

14. K. Rahner, "Christology Within an Evolutionary View of the World," 174–176; and *Foundations of Christian Faith*, 193–194.
15. K. Rahner, *Foundations of Christian Faith*, 195.
16. Ibid., 194–195.

Every self-expression of God that is not simply the beatific vision takes place through a finite reality, through a word or through an event that belongs to the finite, created realm. But as long as this finite mediation of the divine self-expression does not represent the reality of the absolute mystery of God in the strict sense, it is still basically provisional and surpassable because it is finite. In Jesus Christ, however, there is not just any kind of unity or any kind of connection between a human, historical reality and the divine Word. They are intrinsically related because the human reality in Christ is a self-communication of God. In Christ, a human reality is assumed in such a way that the reality of God is communicated to what is assumed. There is an irrevocable union between this human reality and God, a union that eliminates the possibility of separation between the proclamation and the proclaimer, and hence a union that makes the really human proclamation and the offer to us a reality of the absolute mystery of God. This is what is meant by the hypostatic union. The hypostatic union means that in the human reality of Jesus, the absolute salvific will of God, the absolute event of God's self-communication to us along with its acceptance as something effected by God, is a reality of God, unmixed but also inseparable and therefore irrevocable.[17]

The reality of Jesus Christ, in whom God's absolute self-communication to the whole human race is present both as offer and acceptance, therefore is the unsurpassable and definitive offer and acceptance because he is not only established by God but is God. If there is in Christ a human reality graced in such an absolute way, then there is a human reality that belongs absolutely to God and so is really and absolutely the offer of God and its complete acceptance. This Christ is a historical moment in God's saving action exercised in the world. He is a part of the history of the entire cosmos. He is not merely God acting on the world but is part of the universe itself, and in fact its highpoint. He is truly a part of the history of the world, a moment within the evolution of the cosmos. Just as it does in every other human

17. K. Rahner, "Christology Within an Evolutionary View of the World," 176–184.

being, the universe achieves self-presence and an orientation to the mystery of God in him.

When the Word of God became flesh in Jesus Christ, God laid hold of matter in the unity of a spiritually human nature. This matter in Christ Jesus is part of the reality and the history of the cosmos, a part that can never be detached from the unity of the world. The Word of God establishes this part of the world as the Word's own reality. This materiality and this human spirit expresses the Word and allows the Word to be present in the world. God's laying hold of this part of the single material and spiritual reality of the world is the climax of the self-transcendence of the world as a whole.[18]

There is, therefore, an intrinsic and necessary relationship between Jesus Christ and the self-transcendence of the whole spiritual world into God through God's self-communication. The history of the world is present in the absolute Savior, Jesus Christ, in such a way that God's self-communication to all spiritual creatures attains an irrevocable character. Because of this unique and individual history, the presence of God's self-communication to the whole of creation becomes irreversibly manifest. Jesus Christ fulfills the self-transcendence of the entire universe into the mystery of God, and so he is the highpoint of the liturgy of the world.[19]

THE INCARNATE WORD OF GOD

We can also see how Rahner understands Jesus Christ as the highpoint and fulfillment of the liturgy of the world by studying his view of the incarnation.[20] Rahner thinks that the incarnation

18. K. Rahner, *Foundations of Christian Faith*, 195–203.
19. K. Rahner, "Christology Within an Evolutionary View of the World," 184–192.
20. For Rahner's theology of the incarnation, *see* Karl Rahner, "On the Theology of the Incarnation," TI 4 (New York: Crossroad, 1982) 105–120; "Incarnation," *Encyclopedia of Theology: The Concise* Sacramentum Mundi, 690–699; *Foundations of Christian Faith*, 212–228; "The Enfleshment of God," *Spiritual Exercises* (London: Sheed and Ward, 1966) 97–113; "The Eternal Significance of the Humanity of Jesus for Our Relationship with God," TI 3 (New York: Crossroad, 1982) 35–46; and "Thoughts on the Theology of

is frequently understood by Christians in ways that at best border on the mythological and at worst completely distort the meaning of what has been accomplished in Christ. Rahner thinks that most Christians today do not really believe that God became fully human in Jesus Christ. Rather, they presume that the humanity of Jesus was little more than a disguise that God assumed for a brief time. The objective of theologians and pastoral ministers today must be to present the incarnation in ways that will clearly demonstrate that God became fully human.[21]

Rahner thinks that it must be noted from the very beginning that when we discuss God becoming human, we are concerned with the Word of God, the second person of the Trinity. Ever since the time of St. Augustine, it has been assumed that any of the three persons in the Trinity could have become human. When theologians operating under this assumption would speak about the "Word of God" becoming flesh, they meant no more than one of the Trinity became human. An older pre-Augustinian tradition found mainly among the Greek Fathers held that it is precisely the second person of the Trinity who becomes human. This tradition says that only the Word of God can become human in such a way that the incarnate Word is not a creature distinct from God but is the real self-communication of God.[22]

For Rahner, the immanent self-expression of God in the Word makes God's outward self-expression possible. If God expresses God's very own self into what is not God, this expression is the outward expression of God's immanent Word and not something arbitrary that could also be proper to another divine person. Therefore, we can only understand the incarnation if we understand the Word of God. But the converse is equally true: We can

Christmas," TI 3 (New York: Crossroad, 1982) 24–34. *See also* Karl Rahner, "The Quest for Approaches Leading to an Understanding of the Mystery of the God-Man Jesus," TI 13 (New York: Crossroad, 1983) 195–200; "Christmas in the Light of the Ignatian Exercises," TI 17 (New York: Crossroad, 1981) 3–7; "Christmas, the Festival of Eternal Youth," TI 7 (New York: Seabury, 1977) 121–126; "Holy Night," TI 7 (New York: Seabury, 1977) 127–131; and "Peace on Earth," TI 7 (New York: Seabury, 1977) 132–135.

21. K. Rahner, "Thoughts on the Theology of Christmas," 29.

22. K. Rahner, *Foundations of Christian Faith*, 214–215; and "On the Theology of the Incarnation," 106–107.

only understand the Word of God if we understand the incarnation. Rahner's approach is to explore the meaning of the incarnation, the mystery of the Word of God becoming human, by beginning with the question of what it means to be human.[23]

While we have a vast amount of information supplied by the sciences, the arts, and our experience about what it means to be human, none of it can provide us with an exact and comprehensive definition of ourselves. We can never finally define what it means to be human, since we are essentially transcendental subjects who are directed toward the absolute mystery we call God. All our various parts can never be gathered together and encapsulated in a tidy definition, because one of those elements, the one that grounds all the others, is our unlimited transcendentality. We are free to accept or reject our transcendental orientation to God, but we can never escape it. We are inescapably directed toward the God who is incomprehensible. Since we are fundamentally oriented to the absolute mystery of God, our essence or nature is an indefinable mystery. Mystery always and necessarily characterizes God and through God characterizes us.[24]

We fundamentally and inescapably participate in the absolute mystery of God. God always remains incomprehensible, and through our essential transcendentality we will always participate in the mystery of God, even when we are brought together with God in the beatific vision. It is of our very essence to be a mystery because it is of our essence to be transcendent, to be spirit, to be oriented to the absolute mystery.[25]

Not only are we oriented to the mystery of God, we are made to be filled by the mystery of God. The transcendentality of our essence opens us to the possibility of receiving the mystery of God. Our transcendentality is an obediential potency, a positive

---

23. Karl Rahner, *The Trinity* (New York: Seabury, 1974) 28–30; "Divine Trinity," *Encyclopedia of Theology: The Concise* Sacramentum Mundi (New York: Crossroad, 1982) 1755–1764; and "Trinity in Theology," ibid., 1764–1771.

24. Karl Rahner, "What Is Man?" *Christian at the Crossroads* (New York: Seabury, 1975) 11–20; "On the Theology of the Incarnation," 107–109; and *Foundations of Christian Faith*, 215–217.

25. K. Rahner, *Spiritual Exercises*, 99–104.

affinity, for God's self-communication. The fact that we are defined by our essential indefinability, our unlimited openness to the infinite God, makes it possible for us to receive a self-communication from God. This means that our essential openness to the mystery of God can be filled by the absolute mystery of God if God chooses to do so. In fact, our unlimited transcendentality can only be filled by the self-communication of the infinite mystery. Only God can be the unlimited answer for the unlimited question which we are. Only such a self-communication of God can fill our essential openness. An absolute self-communication of the mystery of God would be the highest possible fulfillment of the essence of our humanity.[26]

If human nature is essentially a transcendental openness to God, an openness that would reach its highest completion in an absolute self-communication of the mystery of God, then we can understand more clearly what it means to say that God assumed a human nature. The very meaning of human nature is to be realized and fulfilled by being filled with the mystery of God. If our indefinable nature was assumed by God as God's self-expression, then it has reached its fulfillment.[27]

But the human nature of the incarnate Word of God was not assumed as though it existed prior to being assumed. That would suggest that the human nature and the Word of God were completely distinct and separate realities, somehow tentatively and temporarily united in Christ. If the Word of God had assumed a preexisting human nature, the incarnate Word would not have really become human. The humanity of the Word would be a disguise for God, which would itself disclose nothing at all of God except perhaps secondarily through what the incarnate Word would have to say. But Jesus was more than just another prophet preaching about God. He was the self-revelation of God through his whole humanity and not only through his words, and he can be this only if his humanity is itself the expression of God.[28]

26. K. Rahner, *Foundations of Christian Faith*, 217–218; and "On the Theology of the Incarnation," 109–110.

27. K. Rahner, "On the Theology of the Incarnation," 108–112.

28. Ibid., 112–120; *Foundations of Christian Faith*, 223–224.

This human reality was created by the Word by being assumed and so it was the true self-expression of the Word. The human nature of Christ was what was created when God decided to manifest God's absolute self-communication and its acceptance in an irrevocable and historical way. The human nature of Christ was not a disguise for the Word of God. It was what the Word of God became when it was absolutely communicated to our history. Our human nature became an intrinsic component of God's self-communication in Jesus Christ. It was a reality that was distinct from God yet totally belonged to God as God's self-expression.

"What" Jesus Christ is as the self-expression of the Word and "what" we are is the same. We call it "human nature." The difference between Christ and ourselves is that this "what" in him is spoken as the self-expression of God, and this is not the case with us. But the fact that he in his reality says exactly what we are redeems us and opens us to the freedom of God. Our nature was uniquely fulfilled when the Word of God became human. Our essential openness to the mystery of God was realized and accepted in an unsurpassable way when this human nature was so given to the absolute mystery and so emptied that it became the nature of God. The incarnation was the highest actualization of the essence of human reality.[29]

The incarnate Word of God, then, is the highpoint of the liturgy of the world. Christ fulfills the essential transcendental openness, which always orients us to God and realizes our potential to receive the absolute self-communication of God. Both the human and the divine sides of the liturgy of the world are irreversibly fulfilled in him.

THE LIFE, DEATH, AND RESURRECTION OF CHRIST

In studying the incarnation, we have been engaged in a type of Christology that Rahner calls "metaphysical" or "descending"

29. K. Rahner, *Foundations of Christian Faith*, 215–219, 222–226; "On the Theology of the Incarnation," 115–116; *Spiritual Exercises*, 108–113; "The Eternal Significance of the Humanity of Jesus," 43–46; and "Thoughts on the Theology of Christmas," 29–34.

Christology. That is to say, it is a type of Christology that emphasizes the preexistent Word of God and the assumption of a human reality by the Word. Such an approach tends to consider these matters as being self-evident and explores them with little reference to the life and death of the historical Jesus. While this type of metaphysical Christology is both valid and valuable, we can nonetheless benefit from the saving-history type of Christology. This type of Christology focuses on the historical Jesus of Nazareth. He is seen as the irrevocable and unsurpassable self-communication of God to humanity precisely in his life, death, and resurrection.[30]

We need to investigate Rahner's saving-history Christology at this point, because his understanding of the precise relationship between Jesus Christ and the liturgy of the world is still somewhat vague. The ideas of the absolute Savior and the incarnation show that Christ is the highpoint and the fulfillment of the liturgy of the world. While this conclusion is important, it falls short of the Christian message. What we have seen so far has only indicated that the cosmic liturgy is fulfilled by the life of Jesus Christ because it is the life of the incarnate Word of God. This can give the impression that the concrete details of the life, death, and resurrection of the incarnate Word are of little or no significance. But the Christian message says that it is precisely the death and the resurrection of the historical Jesus of Nazareth that fulfills salvation history. It is not only important that the incarnate Word lived among us, but also that he lived, died, and rose again in a very specific manner.

The question at this point, then, is how the life of Jesus, which was summed up and finalized in his death on the cross, fulfills the liturgy of the world. Our individual participation in the liturgy of the world is necessarily related to these events. This holds true for Christians and non-Christians, theists and atheists, those who lived before Jesus and those who have lived after him. This problem is a variation on the question of the connec-

---

30. K. Rahner, *Foundations of Christian Faith*, 228–235; and "The Two Basic Types of Christology," 215–219. *See also* Karl Rahner, "Remarks on the Importance of the History of Jesus for Catholic Dogmatics," TI 13 (New York: Crossroad, 1983) 201–212.

tion between Jesus and the universality of salvation, since the liturgy of the world is another way of expressing what Rahner means by salvation history. How is it possible to reconcile the proposition that salvation is a possibility for all people everywhere with the proposition that all salvation comes through Jesus Christ and his death and resurrection? This is especially problematic if we maintain that people who lived before Christ, or who have lived since Christ but have had no contact with Christianity, can be saved through Christ. How can it be said that the death and resurrection of Christ "causes" their salvation?

The question has to do with the universal possibility of salvation, not the actual salvation of particular individuals. There is no condition of human life that would allow us to conclude that those who are found in that condition are necessarily in a state of sin, which would always deny them the possibility of salvation. We have direct saving access to God in every conceivable situation of life. This does not mean that we do not need to be converted or to practice faith, hope, and love in order actually to discover the immediate saving presence of God. Such conversion to God, however, can take place either explicitly or implicitly in any conceivable situation. Since this is the case, how can we claim that salvation comes entirely from Jesus Christ? How does the death of Christ (as it is rooted in the incarnation and fulfilled in the resurrection) make salvation universally available?[31]

Salvation is not only redemption by another but also self-redemption. Whenever we freely accept God as the center of our existence, *we* accept God's self-communication. In this sense, then, we redeem ourselves. God's self-communication makes our self-redemption possible, and so we cannot redeem ourselves without God. Nonetheless, it is important to note that we do not merely passively receive salvation but rather actively accept it in

31. K. Rahner, "On the Theology of Worship," 146; and "The One Christ and the Universality of Salvation," TI 16 (New York: Crossroad, 1983) 199–224. *See also* Karl Rahner, "The Death of Jesus and the Closure of Revelation," TI 18 (New York: Crossroad, 1983) 132–142; "History of the World and Salvation-History," TI 5 (New York: Crossroad, 1983) 97–114; and *Foundations of Christian Faith*, 228–285, 305–321.

freedom. Our understanding of the causality involved in the death of Christ must not overlook the exercise of our freedom in the process of salvation.[32]

Nor can the death of Christ be seen as the cause of the uncaused salvific will of God, at least not in the usual way in which we think of a cause. We normally think of a cause as a moral or physical force that brings something about. But in the case of the cross, we must say that Jesus died and rose again because God wills salvation. We cannot say that God wills our salvation because the cross occurred. The cross does not transform the anger and justice of God into mercy and love. Rather, the cross takes place because God freely willed to communicate God's self to the world and overcome its sin. The cross of Christ does not bring about a will to save in God that otherwise would not have existed.[33]

It is clear from the New Testament that the death of Jesus possesses soteriological significance. This is why a theology of redemption based on the incarnation alone is inadequate. Admittedly, Jesus is related to everyone else within the framework of a single humanity and its history. Humanity and history form a genuine unity and are not merely the collection of individual human beings or isolated events. This unity of humanity would be a sufficient basis for explaining the universal significance of Christ if we wanted to say that the redemption was achieved through the incarnation alone. Humanity is one and was saved as a single whole when it was divinized through the incarnation of the Word. But the death of Jesus must possess in itself universal importance for salvation and cannot merely be regarded as an isolated event of no significance in a life that only has universal relevance for salvation simply because it is the life of the eternal Word.[34]

For Rahner, the death of Christ was the definitive act of his freedom, the act in which he summed up his whole life. It is not enough to see death as the separation of the soul and the body.

32. K. Rahner, "The One Christ and the Universality of Salvation," 206–207.
33. Ibid., 207–209.
34. Ibid., 209–211.

Such a view misses the fact that death is something that happens to us as free, spiritual beings. Death is the conclusion of our free personal growth, the supreme act in which we freely gather up our whole lives and possess ourselves. It is neither the end of our existence nor the transition to another mode of existence just as temporal and incomplete as this one. Death is the beginning of eternity insofar as we can speak of eternity having a beginning. It is not only something that happens to us but also a fundamental act of self-realization, the entry into the eternal possession of ourselves.[35]

The kind of causality involved in the death and resurrection of Christ is sacramental causality. This is the type of causality that we have already seen is operative in what Rahner calls a "real symbol." He says that "the cross (together with the resurrection of Jesus) has a primary sacramental causality for the salvation of all men, in so far as it mediates salvation to man by means of salvific grace which is universally operative in the world. It is the sign of this grace and of its victorious and irreversible activity in the world. The effectiveness of the cross is based on the fact that it is the primary sacramental sign of grace."[36]

The cross is the "cause" of the universal possibility of salvation because it is the primary sign of the universal availability of saving grace. In the case of sacramental causality, the sign or symbol and the cause are interrelated. An axiom of sacramental theology since Aquinas has been that sacraments cause grace because they are signs of it and are signs of grace because they cause it. Rahner's theology of the real symbol has explored how this is possible. He does not assume that every sign of a thing can also be its cause. But inasmuch as sacraments are real symbols, they are the social and historical embodiments of grace in which grace becomes effective. To this extent the sacramental symbol is a cause of grace, although the symbol is caused by grace. Sign and grace should not be regarded as two completely

35. Karl Rahner, *On the Theology of Death* (Montreal: Palm Publishers, 1961); "On Christian Dying," TI 7 (New York: Seabury, 1977) 285–293; "Ideas for a Theology of Death," TI 13 (New York: Crossroad, 1983) 169–186; and *Foundations of Christian Faith*, 270–273.
36. K. Rahner, "The One Christ and the Universality of Salvation," 212.

distinct realities set over against each other as cause and effect. They are interrelated and mutually dependent. The sign belongs to the essential actualization of grace, which in this way finds an irreversible and effective historical expression. The sign is brought forth by grace as its real symbol so that grace itself achieves fulfillment.[37]

The cross of Christ is the sacramental cause of the universal possibility of salvation. Salvation is universally available because the loving and forgiving will of God embraces the whole world in every age. The offer of God's divinizing self-communication is addressed to every person's freedom, no matter what his or her situation in life might be. Salvation becomes a real event when we freely respond to the grace of God and accept it either implicitly or explicitly. So there is a salvation history that has been and continues to be hidden throughout the course of ordinary history. That salvation history is hidden because of its ambiguity: ordinary historical events cannot clearly indicate to us whether they are harbingers of salvation or damnation. Furthermore, unless and until there is an irrevocable historical manifestation of God's self-communication that is met by an absolute acceptance on our part, the history of salvation would continue to be ambiguous and unfulfilled. Such an absolute divine self-communication and its acceptance is the highest goal of human history.[38]

This is what has taken place in Jesus Christ. In Christ, the self-communication of God has occurred in such a unique way that Christ became the definitive and irreversible self-gift of God to the world. Christ freely accepted the divine self-gift in such a manner that this acceptance, too, became irreversible, that is, through his death as the definitive culmination of his free actions in history. Through this concrete event, salvation history has been irreversibly directed to salvation and not to damnation. This historically tangible event, therefore, is a real symbol of the salvation of the whole world, and so it possesses the type of causality we call sacramental.

The principle that sign and signified are essentially one, so that the reality signified comes to be in and through the sign, and the

37. Ibid., 212–216.
38. K. Rahner, "History of the World and Salvation-History," 97–114.

sign, in this specific and limited sense, causes the reality signified, applies in a fundamental way to the relationship between
the saving will of God and the cross of Jesus. The cross can and
should be understood in this sense as the cause of the universal
possibility of salvation. The cross of Jesus is the universal primary sacrament of the salvation of the whole world.[39]

The principle of sacramental causality, then, explains how the
death of Christ is related to all humanity. But there is a mutual
relationship between Christ and humanity. Christ is related to all
of humanity, and all of humanity is related to Christ. It is especially important to determine how such a mutual relationship can
exist in the case of those who have never been touched by the
explicit message of Christianity: those who lived before Christ,
non-Christians since then, and all those who have never been
reached by the gospel.

Rahner deals with this problem through his theory of "anonymous Christians." Since salvation cannot be achieved except in
reference to God and to Christ, and since faith is required for
salvation, all who are saved must somehow have a relationship
in faith to God and to Christ. If salvation is universally possible,
that means that at least an implicit faith in Christ is also possible
for those who have had little or no contact with Christianity.
Christ is implicitly but genuinely present in their saving faith.
This does not mean that those realities an anonymous Christian
lacks, such as the explicit profession of Christian faith or baptism, are unimportant for salvation and for being a Christian.
What is more important, however, is that the polytheist, the
atheist in good faith, and the theist outside the revelation of the
Old and New Testaments can all possess not only a relationship
of faith to God's self-revelation but also a genuine relationship to
Jesus Christ and his saving action.[40]

39. K. Rahner, "The One Christ and the Universality of Salvation,"
216–220. *See also* Rahner, "The Death of Jesus and the Closure of Revelation," 132–142.

40. Karl Rahner, "Anonymous Christians," TI 6 (New York: Crossroad,
1982) 390–398; "Observations on the Problem of the 'Anonymous Christian,' " TI 14 (New York: Seabury, 1976) 280–294; and "Anonymous and Explicit Faith," TI 16 (New York: Crossroad, 1983) 52–59.

The relationship between Jesus Christ and the universal possibility of salvation and the relationship between Christ and the liturgy of the world is the same. Christ's death is the primary symbol of that original liturgy, which is coextensive with human history. It is the fullest possible expression of this liturgy, and so it causes that liturgy to achieve all that it symbolizes. The reality and the real symbol that expresses that reality are inseparably related. All people who through their freedom are involved in the liturgy of the world, then, are least implicitly related to that liturgy, which Christ fulfilled on his cross.

We have made little reference to the resurrection in our study of Rahner's Christology and its relationship to his theology of worship. This procedure runs the risk of inadvertently adopting a prejudice operative in our theological tradition, namely, the tendency to slight the resurrection in favor of the incarnation and the death of Christ. But the resurrection is at the very heart of the Christian faith and as such has an important part to play in any theology of worship.[41]

Traditional post-Tridentine theology tended to overlook all the events of the life of Jesus other than the incarnation and the crucifixion. It assumed that these were the concerns of exegesis and piety, not serious theology. The resurrection suffered from the same fate as every other episode from the life of Jesus, since it was not seen to have any particular salvific significance. This

41. *See* Karl Rahner, "Dogmatic Questions on Easter," TI 4 (New York: Crossroad, 1982) 121–133; "On the Spirituality of the Easter Faith," TI 17 (New York: Crossroad, 1981) 8–15; "Jesus' Resurrection," TI 17 (New York: Crossroad, 1981) 16–23; "Experiencing Easter," TI 7 (New York: Seabury, 1977) 159–168; "Encounters with the Risen Christ," TI 7 (New York: Seabury, 1977) 169–176; "He Will Come Again," TI 7 (New York: Seabury, 1977) 177–180; "The Festival of the Future of the World," TI 7 (New York: Seabury, 1977) 181–185; "Resurrection of Christ," *Encyclopedia of Theology: The Concise* Sacramentum Mundi, 1430–1431, 1438–1444; *Foundations of Christian Faith,* 266–282; "Remarks on the Importance of the History of Jesus for Catholic Dogmatics," 201–212; "The Eternal Significance of the Humanity of Jesus for Our Relationship with God," 35–46; and "What Does It Mean Today to Believe in Jesus Christ?" 143–156. *See also* John P. Galvin, "The Resurrection of Jesus in Contemporary Catholic Systematics," *Heythrop Journal* 20 (1979) 125–130.

failure to see any salvific importance in the resurrection points to a deeper problem: Beginning with Tertullian and Cyprian, and then developing in Augustine and Anselm, Western theology adopted a juridical interpretation of the redemption. This approach presupposed that we could only be saved if God received the satisfaction due for the offense caused by our sin. Given the nature of the offense, the required satisfaction was such that only a divine-human person could render it. The sole significance of the incarnation in the economy of salvation is that it brings about the creation of a divine-human person who could render this satisfaction for our sin.[42]

The juridical view assumed that God could have accepted any work of this divine-human person as the work of redemption, but that in fact God chose Christ's death. All the other events of Christ's life are important only as ways in which God prepared for the cross. The only event that has decisive significance for our salvation is the death of Christ. The resurrection was thought to affect only the private destiny of Christ; it was his glorification. In this view the resurrection does not have any direct impact on our salvation. Nor does the humanity of Jesus have any salvific function after the resurrection. It is as if the death of Christ would have saved us even if the resurrection had never happened.

The failure to appreciate what has been accomplished for our salvation in the resurrection can be seen in two contrasting models that Christians have of their relationship with Jesus Christ. In the first model, believers gaze backward into a past that no longer exists. They focus on the actual life of the historical Jesus, from his birth up to his death and resurrection. But the resurrection is seen here merely as the final phase of his historical existence. Such believers take a pilgrimage back in time, as it were, to contemplate the life of Jesus. The historical narrative they focus on is unique, of course. But the mode of access to this narrative is no different than the access they have to the story of any other historical figure. The other model looks upward into the eternity of God outside history. This view focuses on Jesus

42. K. Rahner, "Dogmatic Questions on Easter," 123–124.

as the transfigured Lord in his blessedness and glory. The problem here is that in this adoring relationship to the transfigured Lord, no clear distinction is made between the relationship of the believer to the eternal God and to Jesus Christ. The relationship to Jesus is simply merged into the relationship to the mystery of God, and so the earthly history of Jesus hardly plays any role. It disappears into the past and no longer has any importance in the relationship with the glorified Christ.[43]

Both of these models fail to do justice to the unity between transcendence and history. The first model ignores the fact that because of the resurrection, the history of Jesus has taken on an eternal validity, which makes our access to it different from our access to other historical figures. The second model so focuses on the transcendent and eternal God that it loses sight of the fact that the risen Christ is Jesus of Nazareth. The resurrection involves an indissoluble unity between transcendence and history, and it requires that Christian spirituality and theology recognize this.

The resurrection can only be understood in relationship to the death of Christ. The death of Christ was the definitive, free act in which Christ summed up his whole life. The resurrection of Christ, therefore, is not another event after his passion and death. It is the manifestation of what happened in that death: Christ's absolute self-surrender to the mystery of God and its acceptance by the Father. The cross and the resurrection are two aspects of one event, which are intrinsically and permanently related to one another. The death of Jesus is such that by its very nature it is subsumed into the resurrection. The resurrection does not mean the beginning of a new period in the life of Jesus, a further extension of time filled with new and different things. The resurrection is the confirmation of the single and unique life of Jesus, who achieved the permanently valid and final shape of his life precisely through his death in freedom and obedience. When we turn to the exalted Lord in faith, in hope, and in love, we find none other than the crucified Jesus. The risen Christ is not merely someone who at an earlier time lived a human life,

43. K. Rahner, "On the Spirituality of the Easter Faith," 10–12.

was crucified and died, but has simply left all this behind him as the past and is now leading a different, new life. The risen Lord is the one who was crucified. His earlier life itself is completed and has found eternal reality in and before God.[44]

An awareness of this identity between the earthly Jesus and the exalted Lord corrects the inadequacies of the two models most believers have of their relationship to Christ. The first model overlooks the fact that when we look to the historical Jesus and the events of his life and death, we are seeing the one who has been raised and whose life has taken on a complete and valid form in God. This Jesus is present to us in the "now" of eternity, and so our access to him is different from our access to other historical figures. The second model forgets that when we turn to the glorified Lord, we find the life and history of Jesus of Nazareth. Of course, much in the earthly life of Jesus is simply past and gone and no longer exists; to deny that would be to assert that the history of Jesus is not completed. But since this earthly life of Jesus is completed, it is not after all simply past and gone: It is completed and eternally valid; it has itself been accepted and acknowledged by God. It has been gathered out of the flux of earthly time and taken into eternity.

The resurrection means that the life of Jesus has been completed and has taken on a permanent form. Since this resurrection is the gift of God, the resurrection is the confirmation and vindication of Jesus and his cause. It vindicates the claim Jesus made during his lifetime to be the historical presence of the final and unsurpassable Word of God's self-disclosure. Jesus did not merely proclaim God as the Father who forgives and liberates all sinners and whose grace can transform every human situation no matter how hopeless. Such a proclamation is important for the purity and conviction with which Jesus delivered it. But this message could have been proclaimed without him and does not essentially go beyond the testimony of the Jewish Scriptures in their most profound moments.[45]

44. K. Rahner, "Dogmatic Questions on Easter," 128–129; "Jesus' Resurrection," 21–23; "On the Spirituality of the Easter Faith," 13–15; and *Foundations of Christian Faith*, 266.

45. K. Rahner, "What Does It Mean Today to Believe in Jesus Christ?" 148–151; and *Foundations of Christian Faith*, 250–254, 266–268.

Jesus in fact had a more radical message, which cannot be separated from his person. His proclamation speaks of a new turning of God to humanity in a previously unknown form, a new coming of the kingdom of God. This new coming of the kingdom did not merely represent an offer made to our historical freedom, in which our acceptance or rejection would remain indefinite and so leave history unresolved and open to the possibility of further offers from God and further responses from humanity. Jesus proclaims that this saving offer of God's self-communication is irreversibly victorious and, as irreversibly victorious, becomes historically tangible in him, in his preaching, and then finally in his death. This Jesus, with this concrete claim and his history, is experienced in the resurrection as permanently valid and as accepted by God. This means that salvation has in fact been irreversibly achieved for us.

What happens after the death of Christ, then, is not an event prolonged in time and merely attached to his death. What follows after his death is precisely the definitive form of that which took place in his death. If this is so, the risen Lord must have a real salvific function that abides, otherwise no such salvific function can be attributed to his death itself. The life of the exalted Lord is not a reward for his faithful and generous service. It is the permanent and final form of the soteriological significance of his temporal life. The salvific importance of the resurrection goes far beyond its apologetical value and the personal blessedness it brings to Jesus. In an inseparable unity with the death of Christ, it is the cause of our salvation. Everything that we said above about the death of Christ as the primary sacramental sign of salvation applies equally to the resurrection, since the resurrection is the fulfillment, completion, and ratification of Christ's death.[46]

Christ, as a member of the one humanity, is a permanent part of a world that is physically, spiritually, and morally united. In his death a part of this world that is occupied by the freedom of Christ is surrendered in the total self-mastery that can be achieved only in the act of death in complete obedience and

---

46. K. Rahner, "Dogmatic Questions on Easter," 131–133; and *Foundations of Christian Faith*, 279–280.

love. Christ's resurrection, then, is the irreversible beginning of the transformation of the world. In this beginning, the glorification and divinization of the whole universe is already in principle decided. The resurrection means that the humanity of Jesus was not merely once in the past decisive for our salvation. It is now and permanently the means of our direct access to God. The transfigured human reality of Jesus remains perpetually the mediator of our immediate relationship to God. The traditional doctrine of the eternal liturgy and intercession of Christ in heaven expresses this fact. The glorified humanity of Jesus is the essential mediation of our worship of the Father.[47]

"The risen and exalted Lord must be the permanent and ever-active access to God, which is always being used anew and can never be left as something passed over and past. He must always show the Father. Only when we have understood this, have we understood Easter as it is: the consummation of the world which gives access to God, who is really all in all through the Easter event, which has already begun but is still reaching completion in us. . . . On this basis one might show how every eucharistic celebration is essentially an Easter feast, not merely because it refers back to a 'past' event, but because it is the presence of that which came to be at Easter."[48]

Thus the crucified and risen Lord is and will always remain the source and summit of the liturgy of the world. All true worship is at least an implicit, anonymous participation in Christ's indestructible communion with the absolute mystery. When the Church gathers to celebrate the Eucharist, we explicitly join in his exchange of self-gifts with the Father. Our humanity is united with the glorified humanity of Christ, and we, too, take part in the fulfillment and transformation of the material universe, which began in the resurrection.

47. K. Rahner, *Encyclopedia of Theology: The Concise* Sacramentum Mundi, 1441–1442; "On the Spirituality of the Easter Faith," 15; and "The Eternal Significance of the Humanity of Jesus for Our Relationship with Christ," 44–45.
48. K. Rahner, "Dogmatic Questions on Easter," 132–133.

Chapter Six

The Church and the Liturgy of the World

The basic tenet of Rahner's theology of worship is that the liturgy of the Church is the symbolic manifestation of the liturgy of the world.[1] The Church's worship is not merely a manifestation of the liturgy of the world; it is *the* basic ritual expression of that liturgy, whose source and summit is Jesus Christ. This is another way of saying that the Church is the basic sacrament of the salvation of the world. Because of the Church's unique relationship to Jesus Christ, the Church's worship life is the clearest and most effective symbolic embodiment of the liturgy of the world.

THE NECESSITY OF THE CHURCH

Rahner's understanding of the liturgy of the Church has everything to do with his ecclesiology. But it is not always readily apparent how the Church fits into Rahner's idea of Christianity. His treatment of themes such as human subjectivity, freedom, and the self-communication of God can sometimes give the mistaken impression that Christianity is essentially a phenomenon that concerns individuals in their relationship to God. After all, every individual person is addressed by God's offer of grace and responds to that grace through the exercise of his or her freedom. This self-communication of God becomes an event of salvation for the individual when the individual accepts it as the source and goal of his or her life. Christianity, then, can appear to be a religion that is primarily concerned with the individual's transcendental experience.

This impression can be reinforced by the concept of "anonymous Christians." If there really is such a thing as anonymous

---

1. Karl Rahner, "On the Theology of Worship," TI 19 (New York: Crossroad, 1983) 146.

Christians, if it really is possible for those who have no contact with Christianity to be saved through the grace of Christ, then it might seem that an ecclesial form of Christianity is unnecessary. The Church appears to be something secondary to our relationship with God and the process of salvation. It appears to be no more than a practical organization that is useful, but not necessary, for supporting our transcendental relationship with God. The impression is that nothing essential to Christianity would be lost if there were only anonymous Christians and not ecclesially committed ones.

We have seen that the liturgy of the world is a continual exchange of self-gifts between humanity and the absolute mystery. This process is expressed in a history of ostensibly secular events, which is coextensive with the history of the world, and in a special history of explicitly sacred events. The cosmic liturgy reached its highpoint and fulfillment in Jesus Christ and is ritually celebrated in the liturgy of the Church. But the vast majority of those who in the course of human history have participated in the liturgy of the world have never participated in the liturgy of the Church. It is clear, therefore, that it is not necessary to participate in the Church's worship in order to participate in the liturgy of the world. How, then, can we say that it is necessary for the liturgy of the world to take an ecclesial form? If those who have no contact with Christianity can nevertheless be saved in Christ, and if the liturgy of the world can be expressed in a variety of individual and communal forms, can we maintain that the Church and its liturgy are necessary for Christianity?

The Church is a necessary and essential part of Christianity for Rahner. When Christianity is fully expressed and realized it becomes Church. Something vital to Christianity would be lost if Christians did not embody their communion with one another and become Church. The communal, ecclesial form of Christianity more fully realizes the nature of Christianity than does the individual, anonymous form. If the liturgy of the world is to be fully realized, therefore, it must take the form of an ecclesial worship. The liturgy of the world is necessarily directed toward the kind of social and public expression that it finds in the liturgy of the Church. If the Church's worship ceased to exist, something basic and essential for the liturgy of the world would not be realized.[2]

Rahner thinks that the Church and its worship are necessary because we are essentially interpersonal beings. We receive and become who we are as individuals only in and through our communication with others. The individual and the social dimensions of human existence (like the transcendental and the historical) are mutually dependent and condition one another. Our orientation toward other people is a characteristic that determines our whole existence.[3] So Rahner says:

"A person cannot discover his personhood and his uniqueness by looking for them as something absolutely contrary to his social nature, but can only discover them *within* his social nature and in function of this social nature. . . . Man is a social being, a being who can exist only within such intercommunication with others throughout all of the dimensions of human existence."[4]

The fact that we are essentially and completely social beings determines the process of salvation. Salvation does not just touch limited parts of our lives. If and when we are saved, the saving grace of God embraces us as whole persons. Therefore, Christianity concerns our whole existence, including our interpersonal relationships. Christianity is not about a transcendental relationship that we can live out individually in privacy. The relationships that we have to others necessarily belong to it.[5]

2. For the following *see* Karl Rahner, *Foundations of Christian Faith: An Introduction to the Idea of Christianity* (New York: Seabury, 1978) 322–323, 342–343, 345–346, 347–348, 389–390; "Courage for an Ecclesial Christianity," TI 20 (New York: Crossroad, 1981) 3–12; "Church, Churches and Religions," TI 10 (New York: Seabury, 1977) 30–49; and "The Significance in Redemptive History of the Individual Member of the Church," *The Christian Commitment: Essays in Pastoral Theology* (New York: Sheed and Ward, 1963) 75–113. For a survey of the development of Rahner's ecclesiological writings, *see* Leo O'Donovan, ed., "A Changing Ecclesiology in a Changing Church: A Symposium on Development in the Ecclesiology of Karl Rahner," TS 38 (1977) 736–762.

3. K. Rahner, "The Significance in Redemptive History of the Individual Member of the Church," 75–113.

4. K. Rahner, *Foundations of Christian Faith*, 323.

5. Ibid., 347–348.

"We cannot exclude communal and social intercommunication from man's essence even when he is considered as the religious subject of a relationship to God. If basically God is not a particular reality alongside all other possibilities, but rather is the origin and the absolute goal of the single and total person, then the whole person including his social and interpersonal dimension is related to this God. By the very nature of man and by the very nature of God, and by the very nature of the relationship between man and God when God is understood correctly, the social dimension cannot be excluded from the essence of religion. It belongs to it because man in all of his dimensions is related to the one God who saves the whole person."[6]

If Christianity is to be fully realized in a historical fashion, it must express the fact that we are saved not as isolated individuals but as essentially social beings. That is to say, if Christianity is to be fully realized it must be embodied as Church. Ecclesial community belongs to our religious existence and is coconstitutive of our relationship to God. The Church is not merely an organization for the practice of Christianity, as though Christianity could exist quite independently of it. The Church is part of the real essence of Christianity, and so it has salvific significance. This does not mean that someone who does not belong to the institutional Church cannot be saved in Christ. God's saving grace is offered to everyone and effects the salvation of all who accept it by following the dictates of their consciences. But when Christianity is fully and historically realized, it has an ecclesial shape. The Church, therefore, is a necessary part of Christianity as the event of salvation. Communal and social intercommunication cannot be excluded from our essence when we consider our relationships to God, and so the social dimension cannot be excluded from the essence of Christianity. It belongs to it because we are related in all of our dimensions to the one God who saves the whole person.[7]

6. Ibid., 343. See also Wendelin Knoch, "Das Heil des Menschen in seiner ekklesiologischen Dimension," Wagnis Theologie, hrsg. H. Vorgrimler (Freiburg: Herder, 1979) 487–498.

7. K. Rahner, Foundations of Christian Faith, 342–346, 389–390; and "Church, Churches and Religions," 38–45.

This social dimension of the process of salvation would be lost if Christianity failed to assume an ecclesial form. This is why the Church is necessary if Christianity is to be fully realized. Likewise, the communal form of worship is necessary and essential for the full symbolic manifestation of the liturgy of the world, because that liturgy of the world is essentially social. We participate in the liturgy of the world as social beings, and if the symbolic expression of that liturgy is to be complete it must take a social form. This is not to say that individual and private forms of prayer and worship are secondary or superfluous.[8] On the contrary, the individual and communal forms of worship are mutually dependent and condition one another. Rahner says that "even the most private prayer must and can be prayed from within the one and common salvation situation which consists in God's approach to the one humanity and the one history of men in his Holy Spirit, and in that one history concerns the individual with the uniqueness of his personal history of freedom and responsibility. Common liturgical prayer, however, is prayer and not mere ritualism only when the individual really prays in the community, when he really places himself before God as this individual."[9]

For Rahner, then, we can and should express our experience of the liturgy of the world through our individual practices of prayer. But communal worship is necessary and essential because only it can express the fact that the liturgy of the world embraces our lives as social beings. The clearest and best symbolic manifestation of the liturgy of the world will have a ecclesial form. The only complete symbolic manifestation of our communion with one another and with God in history will be the kind of communion that takes place when the Church gathers to worship.

8. *See* Karl Rahner, "The Prayer of the Individual and the Liturgy of the Church," *Grace in Freedom* (New York: Herder and Herder, 1969) 137–181.

9. Karl Rahner, "The Possibility and Necessity of Prayer," *Christian at the Crossroads* (New York: Seabury, 1975) 59.

The Church's worship is the best symbolic expression of the liturgy of the world, not only because it is a communal form of ritual activity but because the Church has a unique relationship to Jesus Christ, the highpoint and fulfillment of the cosmic liturgy. The liturgy of the Church is the basic symbolic manifestation of the liturgy of the world, precisely because the Church is the basic sacrament of Christ.

This unique relationship between Christ and the Church has traditionally been expressed by saying that Jesus of Nazareth "instituted" the Church.[10] But our understanding of the institution of the Church by Jesus was challenged in this century when theological scholarship made two points clear: that the historical Jesus had an expectation of the imminent arrival of the eschatological kingdom of God and that Christianity of the New Testament period was organized in a variety of forms. In light of these facts, it became difficult to maintain that the historical Jesus could have clearly intended to found a Church that would continue long after his death in the specific institutional form that it eventually assumed in the West. In other words, it seemed that the Church was unintended by Jesus and therefore of secondary importance for Christianity. In view of Jesus' expectation of the imminent arrival of the kingdom of God, then, is it possible to say that the Church has its origin in Jesus Christ and so has a necessary connection with him?

Rahner prefers to avoid the term "institution" (*Stiftung*) in this context because of its juridical overtones and to speak instead of the origin (*Herkunft*) of the Church.[11] His position is that the Church has its origin in the death and resurrection of Jesus, since through his death and resurrection the self-communication

10. For the following *see* Karl Rahner, "The Church's Redemptive Provenance from the Death and Resurrection of Jesus," TI 19 (New York: Crossroad, 1983) 24–38; and *Foundations of Christian Faith*, 326–335. *See also* Francis S. Fiorenza, "Seminar on Rahner's Ecclesiology: Jesus and the Foundations of the Church—An Analysis of the Hermeneutical Issues," PCTSA 33 (1978) 229–254.
11. K. Rahner, "The Church's Redemptive Provenance from the Death and Resurrection of Jesus," 29.

of God and its acceptance have been manifested as finally and permanently victorious over the sin of the world.[12]

We have already explored the significance of Jesus' death and resurrection. We have seen that throughout the history of the world, God has been ceaselessly communicated to the world in forgiving, divinizing grace as an offer made to our freedom. But because God's self-communication is always offered and never imposed, the ambivalence of our freedom left the ultimate fate of the human race and the universe in doubt. Whether we would finally and definitively accept the salvation offered by our God remained an open question. God brought about salvation in Jesus Christ, because through his death and resurrection this open and ambivalent history of salvation does in fact have a definitely good outcome. The fate of any individual person remains open and unclear, but by the power of God the fate of the world as a whole is given a positive outcome. The crucified and risen Jesus is the permanent promise of God's self-communication to the world, no longer just as an open offer but as a promise that is in fact definitively victorious.

But the crucified and risen Jesus can only be the definitive salvation of the entire world if the victorious self-offering of God is permanently present in the world. Christ Jesus can only exist as God's self-promise to the world if there is a community of faith that believes in him as the final and unsurpassable source of salvation. There must be a community that attests to the permanent presence of God's victorious self-communication in the world. And so Rahner says: "The Church as eschatologically definitive and nevertheless historical, as a community of faith, is the permanent presence precisely of this eschatological and eschatologically victorious self-promise of God to the world in Jesus Christ. And he is what he is only if this community of faith is always there in the world, to make sure that he remains historically as God's eschatological promise to the world."[13]

12. Ibid., 30; and *Foundations of Christian Faith,* 327–331.
13. K. Rahner, "The Church's Redemptive Provenance from the Death and Resurrection of Jesus," 32.

The Church, then, has its origin in the death and resurrection of Jesus inasmuch as they constitute the definitive event of salvation, which resolves the ambivalence of the history of salvation. Such a permanently effective and victorious event of salvation is possible through the death and resurrection of Jesus only if there is a community of faith through which the crucified and risen Jesus continues to be permanently present. In this sense the Church is necessary, for Christ would not be what he is if such a Church did not exist. The self-communication of God has been irrevocably given to the world for its salvation in Jesus Christ, and so the Church exists as the permanent historical manifestation of God's definitive self-promise. The meaning and importance of the Church follows directly from the fact that it is the permanent presence in the world of the crucified and risen Jesus. This central truth of ecclesiology explains the relationship of the Church to the liturgy of the world.

We have already seen how Rahner considers Jesus Christ as the source and summit of the liturgy of the world precisely in and through his death and resurrection. Another way of saying that the Church is the permanent presence in the world of this crucified and risen Jesus is to say that the Church is the permanent presence in the world of the fulfillment of the liturgy of the world. This relationship to Christ, then, is what distinguishes the Church's liturgy from every other celebration of the liturgy of the world. When the Church celebrates its liturgy, it celebrates it as the community of faith, through which the highpoint of the liturgy of the world is permanently present.

This allows the Church to symbolically embody the liturgy of the world in an absolutely unique fashion. We need the liturgy of the Church precisely because we need to have the liturgy of the world symbolically expressed in as complete a fashion as possible. The liturgy of the Church is no substitute for the liturgy of the world. The cosmic liturgy is the original, basic way in which we achieve communion with God. But neither is the liturgy of the world a substitute for the liturgy of the Church. By symbolically incarnating the cosmic liturgy, the Church's worship gives us a unique access to a far deeper communion in Christ.

The themes we have been discussing find their clearest expression in Rahner's understanding of the Church as the basic sacrament. The Church is the basic sacrament of God's victorious grace because it is the abiding sign of Christ's grace-giving presence in the world. The sacramental worship activities of the Church are the concrete expressions of the Church as the basic sacrament of redemptive grace. They are the occasions in which the Church realizes its nature as the basic, ongoing manifestation of the liturgy of the world. This is why the liturgy of the Church is the clearest and most effective symbolic manifestation of the liturgy of the world.[14]

Rahner's view of the Church as the basic sacrament is a development of his understanding of salvation history. We have seen that the official, public history of salvation is the process by which the liturgy of the world, that is, the history of salvation and grace, which pervades the world and human life, becomes explicitly and historically tangible. This universal and collective history of the salvation of all humanity has entered into its final and irreversible phase through Jesus Christ and his death and resurrection. Since Christ and through Christ, grace is no longer merely in the world as an offer but is also in fact triumphantly

---

14. For the following *see* Karl Rahner, *The Church and the Sacraments* (New York: Herder and Herder, 1963) 9–24, 76–117; *Foundations of Christian Faith*, 411–413, 429–430; ''Considerations on the Active Role of the Person in the Sacramental Event,'' TI 14 (New York: Seabury, 1976) 179–184; ''What Is a Sacrament?'' TI 14 (New York: Seabury, 1976) 142–148; ''Personal and Saramental Piety,'' TI 2 (Baltimore: Helicon, 1966) 119–127; and ''Dogmatic Notes on 'Ecclesiological Piety,' '' TI 5 (New York: Crossroad, 1983) 356–365. *See also* Walter Kasper, ''Die Kirche als universales Sakrament des Heils,'' *Glaube in Prozess: Christsein nach dem II Vatikanum, Für Karl Rahner*, hrsg. E. Klinger und K. Wittstadt (Freiburg: Herder, 1984) 221–239; Karl Neumann, ''Diasporakirche als sacramentum mundi. Karl Rahner und die Diskussion um Volkskirche—Gemeindekirche,'' TThZ 91 (1982) 52–71; and Alois Spindeler, ''Kirche und Sakramente. Ein Beitrag zur Diskussion mit Karl Rahner im Blick auf das Tridentinum,'' ThGL 53 (1963) 1–15.

Note that in *The Church and the Sacraments*, Rahner uses the term ''*Ursakrament*'' (original sacrament) to describe the Church. In his later writings he reserves that term for Christ and calls the Church the ''*Grundsakrament*'' (basic sacrament).

there. The world is saved as a whole because God brings about in Christ that the world wills to be saved. Jesus Christ is the historically real and actual presence of the eschatologically victorious mercy of God.

Viewed in relation to Christ, the historically visible Church is the real symbol of his abiding presence as the saving grace of God in the world. It is the symbol which brings to manifestation at the historical level and thereby also "effects" the presence of Christ. So there exists between the Church and Christ the same reciprocal relationship that exists between a real symbol and what it symbolizes. The Church as a real symbol remains distinct from what it symbolizes, Christ, but it is the way in which Christ expresses himself and renders himself present in the world. The fact that the Church is constituted along juridically established lines, that it has its social and freely chosen aspects, does not mean that it is merely an arbitrary sign and not a reality symbolic in itself of the presence of Christ and his definitive work of salvation in the world.[15]

Since the Church is the permanent presence of the crucified and risen Jesus in the world, it is not merely a social and juridical entity. The Church as a symbol of the grace of God in Christ really contains what it symbolizes. Viewed in relation to its worship activities, it is the primary sacrament of the grace of God, not merely designating but also really possessing in a fashion analogous to the incarnation what was brought definitively into the world by Christ, the irrevocable grace of God, which conquers humanity's guilt. So the Church is the basic symbol of that triumphant highpoint of the liturgy of the world, which was reached in the death and resurrection of Christ.[16] Rahner says,

"As the ongoing presence of Jesus Christ in time and space, as the fruit of salvation which can no longer perish, and as the means of salvation by which God offers his salvation to an individual in a tangible way and in the historical and social dimen-

15. K. Rahner, *The Church and the Sacraments*, 9–19; and "Dogmatic Notes on 'Ecclesiological Piety,'" 356–365.
16. K. Rahner, *Foundations of Christian Faith*, 411–413, 429–430; and "Personal and Sacramental Piety," 119–127.

sion, the Church is the basic sacrament. This means that the Church is a *sign* of salvation, and is not simply salvation itself. But insofar as the Church is the continuation of God's self-offer in Jesus Christ in whom he has the final, victorious and salvific word in the dialogue between God and the world, the Church is an *efficacious* sign. . . . The Church is the sign and the historical manifestation of the victorious success of God's self-communication. . . . And to this extent the Church is a sign, but it is the sign of an *efficacious* and successful grace for the world, and it is the basic sacrament in this radical sense."[17]

As the basic sacrament of the grace of God, the Church is the real symbol of salvation for the world. It is not simply, or even primarily, the sacrament of salvation for its own members but is the social and historical symbol of salvation of all who are sanctified and redeemed by grace. It is this because the Church constitutes the visible community of those who acknowledge that salvation is victoriously present for the whole world through Christ. As this, the Church brings to manifestation on the historical level and thereby "effects" that grace that is already present in the innermost heart of the world and of the whole of human life. It is the historical realization of the fundamental liturgical drama that lies at the center of the world and its history.[18]

The individual sacraments are concrete acts of self-fulfillment on the part of the Church as the primary sacrament of the liturgy of the world. The abiding, indestructible union of the Church with Christ that is the Church's as the basic sacrament is concretized whenever an ecclesial community celebrates its sacraments. These worship activities designate the same grace that the basic sacrament of the Church designates: that grace that is present and effective within the world constantly. They are not extrinsic processes touching upon an unhallowed world from without but manifestations of the grace operative in the world.[19]

17. K. Rahner, *Foundations of Christian Faith*, 412.

18. K. Rahner, "Considerations on the Active Role of the Person in the Sacramental Event," 179–180; and "What Is a Sacrament?" 142–144.

19. K. Rahner, *The Church and the Sacraments*, 20–24, 76–117; "Considerations on the Active Role of the Person in the Sacramental Event," 181–184; and "What Is a Sacrament?" 144–148.

The individual sacraments must be understood from the perspective of the Church as the basic symbol of the liturgy of the world.[20] A sacrament is present when "the Church involves itself absolutely and exercises one of its basic acts, an act in which it actualizes its essence fully as the primordial sacrament of grace, and actualizes it upon an individual in a situation which is decisive for his salvation."[21]

For Rahner, a genuine sacrament is an action in which the Church realizes and manifests its nature as the basic sacrament of the liturgy of the world. Sacraments are directed to individuals in situations that are important for salvation. So each sacrament must be understood on the one hand from the perspective of the Church and on the other hand from the perspective of the history of our individual lives.

In baptism we become Christians and members of the Church. It is the first sacrament of the forgiveness of sins, the self-communication of God that gives us the capacity to practice faith, hope, and love. Baptism is this because in baptism we are received into the community of those who believe in and profess God's salvation in Christ. We receive the Holy Spirit in baptism precisely by being made members of the Church.[22]

---

20. In addition to the sources mentioned in previous sections, see Karl Rahner, *Meditations on the Sacraments*, (New York: Seabury, 1977); "Glaube und Sakrament," STh 16 (Einsiedeln: Benziger, 1984) 387–397; "Fragen der Sakramententheologie," STh 16 (Einsiedeln: Benziger, 1984) 398–405; and "Introductory Observations on Thomas Aquinas' Theology of the Sacraments in General," TI 14 (New York: Seabury, 1976) 149–160. The important secondary literature on Rahner's sacramental theology includes Manfred Köhnlein, *Was bringt das Sakrament? Disputation mit Karl Rahner* (Göttingen, 1971); Pius Künzle, "Sakramente und Ursakramente," FZPhTh 10 (1963) 428–444; Peter Hünermann, "Reflexionen zum Sakramentenbegriff des II Vatikanums," *Glaube in Prozess*, hrsg. E. Klinger und K. Wittstadt (Freiburg: Herder, 1984) 309–324; Hans-Joachim Schulz, "Karl Rahners Sakramententheologie: Zugang zu Ostkirche und Ökumene," *Wagnis Theologie*, hrsg. H. Vorgrimler (Freiburg: Herder, 1979) 402–416; and Geoffery Wainwright, "Sacramental Theology and the World Church," PCTSA 39 (1984) 69–83.

21. K. Rahner, *Foundations of Christian Faith*, 417–418.

22. Ibid., 415; and *The Church and the Sacraments*, 87–90.

The fact that we receive grace for our own salvation in baptism insofar as we become members of the Church does not mean, however, that the Church membership conferred in baptism exists solely to provide us with justification and sanctification. Membership in the Church is not only a means of attaining our individual salvation. While the Church is useful and important for this purpose, the salvation of individuals is often achieved without any tangible intervention by the Church. The purpose of the Church is also to make the presence of the grace of God in Christ historically and socially tangible in the world. When we are baptized into this community, we receive a mandate and the capacity to participate in this function of the Church. We are appointed by baptism to be representatives of the grace of Christ in the world.[23]

Confirmation should be seen together with baptism as part of a single process of Christian initiation, which is extended in time. Baptism highlights our participation in the death of Christ and incorporation into the Church. Confirmation emphasizes the social and functional aspect of baptism. The grace of confirmation is the grace of the Church for its mission to the world and for proclaiming the world's transfiguration.[24]

In the sacrament of orders not only are the offices of the Church handed on, but the recipients of those offices are sanctified. While it is true that there can be a separation of power in office from holiness in office in individual cases, that is not the case for office as a whole in the Church. If the Church is to remain the presence of the victorious grace of Christ, then the Church's offices must be preserved by God in holiness. The efficacy of a sacrament when it is celebrated is not dependent on the holiness of the minister, but the existence and continuation

23. K. Rahner, *Foundations of Christian Faith*, 415–416; "Taufe und Taufer-neuerung," STh 16 (Einsiedeln: Benziger, 1984) 406–417; and "The Sacramental Basis for the Role of the Layman in the Church," TI 7 (New York: Seabury, 1977) 51–74.

24. K. Rahner, *Foundations of Christian Faith*, 416–417; and *The Church and the Sacraments*, 90–93.

of sacraments in the Church is dependent on the holiness of office as a whole in the Church.[25]

The sacrament of matrimony is a moment in the self-actualization of the Church because it is performed by two baptized Christians who do precisely what is specific to the Church: They are a sign of love that manifests the gracious love that unites God and humanity. Conversely, this very same grace that unites God and humanity is manifested in the unity between Christ and the Church. This manifestation, because it is the absolute goal of God's self-communication, is the ground of all other grace and its unifying function in the world. So the unity in the love of two people is conditioned by the unity between Christ and the Church. The former exists because the latter exists.[26]

The Church is the basic sacrament of God's unconditional and irrevocable word of forgiveness in Jesus Christ. The Church articulates this word of forgiveness in its preaching, in baptism, and in its prayer. The sacrament of penance takes place when this word is addressed to us as baptized Christians, upon the confession of our guilt, by a representative of the Church who has been expressly designated for this. By our sins we place ourselves in contradiction to the holy community to which we belong. Hence in the sacrament of penance, the Church also forgives the injustice that we do to the Church. The Church forgives sin *by* forgiving the injustice we have done to the Church,

25. K. Rahner, *Foundations of Christian Faith*, 417–419; *The Church and the Sacraments*, 95–106; "The Point of Departure in Theology for Determining the Nature of the Priestly Office," TI 12 (New York: Seabury, 1974) 31–38; "How the Priest Should View His Official Ministry," TI 14 (New York: Seabury, 1976) 202–219; and "On the Diaconate," TI 12 (New York: Seabury, 1974) 61–80. *See also* George Linbeck, "Sacramentality of the Ministry: Karl Rahner and a Protestant View," *Oecumencia* (1967) 282–301; and Herlinde Pissarek-Hudelist, "Die Bedeutung der Sakramententheologie Karl Rahners für die Diskussion um das Priestertum der Frau," *Wagnis Theologie*, hrsg. H. Vorgrimler (Freiburg: Herder, 1979) 417–434.

26. K. Rahner, *Foundations of Christian Faith*, 419–421; *The Church and the Sacraments*, 107–112; and "Marriage as a Sacrament," TI 10 (New York: Seabury, 1977) 199–221.

just as it communicates the Holy Spirit of the Church to us in baptism *by* incorporating us into the Church.[27]

Serious sickness creates decisive situations in our individual salvation histories. In these situations we are forced to come to terms with ourselves and with God. The sacrament of the sick provides the Church with an opportunity to gather around those who are in this situation and effectively embody the grace of God in Christ.[28]

The Eucharist is a manifestation of the basic sacrament of the Church in the most radical sense. The "effect" of the Eucharist is not only the participation of the individual Christian in the life of Jesus Christ. The effect of the Eucharist is also and especially social and ecclesiological. In the Eucharist, the irrevocable salvific will of God becomes present, tangible, and visible in this world insofar as the tangible and visible community of believers is formed by the Eucharist into the symbol of that grace and its permanence. The Eucharist is the sacrament of the most radical and real presence of the Lord and the fullest actualization of the essence of the Church.[29] "And insofar as everyone participates in the same meal of Christ, who is the giver and the gift at the

27. K. Rahner, *Foundations of Christian Faith*, 419–423; *The Church and the Sacraments*, 93–95; "Zur Situation des Bußsakramentes," STh 16 (Einsiedeln: Benziger, 1984), 418–437; "Forgotten Truths Concerning the Sacrament of Penance," TI 2 (Baltimore: Helicon, 1963) 135–174; "Problems Concerning Confession," TI 3 (Baltimore: Helicon, 1967) 190–206; "The Meaning of Frequent Confession of Devotion," TI 3 (Baltimore: Helicon, 1967) 177–189; "Penance as an Additional Act of Reconciliation with the Church," TI 10 (New York: Seabury, 1977) 125–149; and *Penance in the Early Church*, TI 15 (New York: Crossroad, 1982). *See also* Marlies Mügge, "Entwicklung und theologischer Kontext der Bußtheologie Karl Rahners," *Wagnis Theologie*, hrsg. H. Vorgrimler (Freiburg: Herder, 1979) 435–450.

28. K. Rahner, *Foundations of Christian Faith*, 423–424; and *The Church and the Sacraments*, 112–117.

29. K. Rahner, *Foundations of Christian Faith*, 424–427; *The Church and the Sacraments*, 82–87; *The Celebration of the Eucharist*, with A. Haussling, (New York: Herder and Herder, 1968); "The Eucharist and Our Daily Lives," TI 7 (New York: Seabury, 1977) 211–226; "The Word and the Eucharist," TI 4 (Baltimore: Helicon, 1966) 253–286; "The Eucharist and Suffering," TI 3 (New York: Crossroad, 1982) 161–170; and "Eucharistiche Anbetung," STh 16 (Einsiedeln: Benziger, 1984) 300–304.

same time, the Eucharist is also the sign, the manifestation and the most real actualization of the Church insofar as the Church is and makes manifest the ultimate unity of all men in the Spirit, a unity which has been founded by God in grace."[30]

Through the sacramental worship activities of the Church, the living symbol that is the Church is expressed and realized. The sacraments embody the Church and by doing so embody Christ, the source and summit of the cosmic liturgy. That original liturgical drama, which is the secret ingredient of our history and our daily lives, unfolds in our liturgical assemblies in all its depth and richness. Christ is irrevocably united with the Church, and so the liturgy of the world, which Christ fulfilled, is inseparable from the liturgy of the Church.

WORD AND SACRAMENT

Rahner develops his theology of sacramental worship not only in the context of his understanding of the Church as the basic sacrament but also in light of his theology of the word of God. The liturgy of the world is God's dialogue with humanity, a dialogue which climaxed in the death and resurrection of the incarnate Word of God and which continues in the life of the Church. Rahner thinks that Catholic and Protestant theologians can find grounds for a common discussion of worship in the distinctive theological character of the word of God uttered in the Church, since all Christian confessions agree that the word of God pronounced in the Church has in principle an exhibitive character.[31]

When Rahner says that the word of God has an exhibitive character, he means that the self-communication of God is actually brought about through it. The word of God is addressed to

30. K. Rahner, *Foundations of Christian Faith*, 427.
31. For the following *see* K. Rahner, "What Is a Sacrament?" 135–141; "The Word and the Eucharist," 253–286; *Foundations of Christian Faith*, 427–429; and "Personal and Sacramental Piety," 112–131. *See also* Wilhelm Breuning, "Zum Verhältnis von Wort und Sakrament," *Glaube im Prozess*, hrsg. E. Klinger und K. Wittstadt (Freiburg: Herder, 1984) 418–430; and Luis Maldonado, "Wort und Sakrament in der neueren Entwicklung der Pastoral," *Wagnis Theologie*, hrsg. H. Vorgrimler (Freiburg: Herder, 1979) 393–401.

us in ways that bring about salvation in us. Roman Catholic theology during and since the Second Vatican Council has explicitly said that in the proclamation of the word itself a genuine presence of the Lord, which brings about salvation, is achieved. Rahner sees the sacraments as the highest expression of the word of grace in the Church. A sacrament may be defined as the word of God uttered to the individual by the Church and in the Church in situations that are decisive for the individual's salvation.

The word of God here means the word of God as it appears in the preaching of the Church. The word of God, while it is preserved in the Church in its character as the word of God, is also a human word spoken by individuals who are charged by the Church to preach this word. But salvation is a work of God that is not totally identifiable with the word of God that comes in human words. God's salvific action on us in grace renews us interiorly by making it possible for us to participate in the divine nature. We participate in this renewal by free, personal consent, but such consent must be brought about by God. This prevenient grace of God is an enlightenment and inspiration, and, hence, it is by definition "word," that is, a spiritual self-communication of God to us.

This inward self-communication of God, however, cannot alone be adequate for the normal and fully developed act of its acceptance. If we are essentially and primordially beings in a community, then knowledge of God's grace cannot be adequately given by our inner experience of grace alone; it must also come to us from without. This means that the proclamation of the word of God, insofar as it is conveyed by the historical, external salvific act of God and by the community of believers, belongs necessarily to the inner moments of God's salvific action on us.

As an inner moment of this salvific action of God, the word shares in the special character of the salvific action of God in Christ and the Church. The inner word of grace and the external, historical, social word of revelation are essentially connected and directed to one another. For the full normal accomplishment of the personal self-disclosure of God to us, the inner word of grace and the external, historical word come together as the mutually complementary moments of the one word of God to us. This one word of God to us is part of God's self-revelation, and so it participates inevitably in the character of the salvific action of God in Christ. All assertions about God's salvific activity are of their nature assertions about the word of God, understood as twofold in the unity of the inner and the outward word.

This word of God is the word that brings with it what it affirms. It is itself, therefore, a salvific event, which in its outward, historical, and social form displays what happens in it and under it and brings about what it displays. It renders the grace of God present, because apart from grace it would not really be the word of God in any real sense. The word of God in the strictest sense can exist at all only as an event of grace. Hence, it must have an exhibitive character; it must be a saving event. For the grace in which alone it can be heard and responded to is at the same time the reality of salvation. The word of God in the Church, then, in its full, original sense is not to be taken as a set of doctrinal propositions or intellectual descriptions of something that exists and is available completely independently of this doctrinal instruction. It is not a human word about God. It is a revelatory and actualizing word in which the grace of God is present. The relationship between the word and the grace designated is a reciprocal relationship: The word is formed by the grace that thus comes, and the grace comes by making itself thus audible.

For example, God's offer of the grace of repentance infallibly takes place in sinners if they accept this word in faith and love when they hear the word of the Church calling them to repentance. Therefore, in this preaching of the word of God, that which is preached takes on the character of an event. The grace of God is not merely spoken of but takes place as an event in this utterance. The preached word is an efficacious proclamation that brings about that of which it speaks.

This efficacious dialogue with God takes place in the Church in essentially varying degrees of concentration and intensity. The grace of God always strives for a single, all-embracing goal: that the self-communication of God should be completely given to us in our total acceptance of God's self-surrendering love. But this single and absolute goal of grace is only reached by stages in individuals, who are involved in history and so achieve the single totality of their lives only by a gradual process. The dialogue between God and humanity can only realize its essence in a historical process. It is not always and at every moment fully its whole self: It grows and becomes what it is and must be. It can have its deficient, provisional, and preparatory moments as well as its supreme moments.

The sacraments can be understood as the highest stages of the word of God in the Church. Since grace is the free personal self-communication of God, its disclosure is always free and personal and, hence, essentially word. The sacraments, therefore, must have the character of the word. In the relationship of matter and form in the sacraments, the material element in the sacrament is not the decisive element. In the case of strictly supernatural realities, a purely natural object can never function as a symbol in such a way that the supernatural reality could be attained through it alone. A natural reality can be a symbol of a strictly supernatural reality only when our spiritual, transcendental openness and orientation becomes an intrinsically constitutive element of the symbol. The supernatural reality can display itself only through the medium of the human word. So in the sacraments, the word is necessarily and inevitably the decisive element. A natural object manifests the supernatural here by being absorbed into this utterance of the word. The sacraments are the supreme realizations of the efficacious, salvific word of God in the Church in situations decisive for our salvation.

The dialogue between God and humanity, which has gone on quietly throughout human history, finds its most effective ritual expression in the sacramental worship life of the Church. Especially in the Eucharist, God's word of love and our word of praise are symbolically manifested in such a way that they join together and become one Word: Christ. The dialogue that is embodied in the liturgy of the Church should not be confused with the dialogue that takes place through our history and our world; they are distinct. The liturgy of the world is the original dialogue, the dialogue that was fulfilled in Christ. The value and necessity of the liturgy of the Church lies in the fact that it is not the original liturgy. It allows us to hear that original dialogue more clearly and so to enter into it more deeply. But neither should our dialogue with God in sacramental worship be separated from the liturgy of the world; they condition one another. The dialogue that is implicit in our daily lives and the dialogue that becomes explicit in our liturgical assemblies are mutually dependent.

THE SACRAMENTS AND GRACE

The mutual dependence of the liturgy of the Church and the liturgy of the world is an expression of the mutual dependence of sacraments and grace. The question of how sacraments cause grace has preoccupied sacramental theologians for centuries. The question itself was the product of the tendency of medieval theologians to treat the sacraments, grace, and God as distinct (and almost material) realities. Consequently, sacramental causality came to be seen in terms of a transitive efficient causality, a type of causality in which one thing distinct from another must produce the latter. When the causality of the sacramental sign was thought of in relation to God, it was seen as a *causalitas moralis*, that is, as the making good of a legal claim on someone who has contracted to perform something. And when the causality of the sacramental sign was thought of in terms of grace, it was seen as a *causalitas physica*, the physical causation of an effect. Since the rite obviously cannot "physically" cause grace, this view saw the causality in question as instrumental: The rite causes a spiritual effect because it is an instrument in God's hand. The sacraments' function as signs and their function as causes were linked in purely extrinsic fashion. The axiom that was often quoted, *sacramenta significando efficiunt gratiam*, was not in fact taken seriously.[32]

Rahner says that the appropriate way to see the intrinsic connection between the sign and the cause in the sacraments is to treat the sacraments as real symbols. The fact that the sacraments are real symbols follows from the fact that the Church is a real symbol. The Church is the presence, embodiment, and manifestation of God's eschatologically triumphant grace in Jesus

32. K. Rahner, *The Church and the Sacraments*, 34–40.

Christ. Therefore, the Church is the symbol, in the fullest sense of that word, of the abiding presence of Christ in the world. Viewed in relation to the sacraments, the Church is the primal and fundamental sacrament of God's grace. The sacraments, in turn, make concrete and actual for the life of the individual person this symbolic reality of the Church as the primary sacrament. Therefore, the sacraments are also symbolic realities, in keeping with the nature of the Church. They are real symbols of God's efficacious grace in the Church. The basic axiom of traditional sacramental theology, *sacramenta efficiunt quod significant et significant quod efficiunt*, points to that mutually supportive relationship that exists between a real symbol and what is symbolized.[33]

The special kind of causality involved in the sacraments, therefore, is symbolic causality. Rahner's theology of real symbols is central to his theology of sacramental worship. There is an intrinsic and mutually causal relationship between the symbol and what is symbolized. On the one hand, that which is symbolized causes the symbol by realizing itself in the symbol as in a reality distinct from itself. And on the other hand, the symbol is the cause of the fact that that which is symbolized is realized as present and operative. In other words, the symbol is a cause of what it symbolizes by being the way in which that which is symbolized effects itself. This mutually causal relationship means that the symbol and what is symbolized are intrinsically related and cannot be adequately understood apart from each other.[34]

This is the case with sacraments. There is an intrinsic and mutually causal relationship between sacraments and grace. They cannot be understood apart from each other. On the one hand, the sacraments are causes of grace because they are its symbols, and on the other hand they are symbols of grace because they are its cause. The Church in its visible historical form is itself a symbol of the eschatologically triumphant grace of God in Christ. Christ acts through the Church in regard to an individual person

33. K. Rahner, *Foundations of Christian Faith*, 411–413; and "What Is a Sacrament?" 142–144.
34. Karl Rahner, "The Theology of the Symbol," TI 4 (Baltimore: Helicon, 1966) 221–252.

by manifesting the gift of his grace in the sacraments. The sacraments are the symbols of God's action on us in Christ and through the Church.

It is impossible to ask whether the sacraments "work" on God and cause grace by "physical" or "moral" causality precisely because the sacraments are symbolic realities, which the grace of God itself brings about in order to be present. The grace, which comes from God, is the cause of the sign, bringing it about and so alone making itself present. The grace of God constitutes itself actively present in the sacraments by creating their expression, which is its own symbol. At the same time, the sacrament is precisely the cause of grace, inasmuch as it is its symbol and the way in which the grace becomes present and effective.[35]

In other words, the liturgy of the Church is the symbol of the liturgy of the world precisely because it is its cause, and it is its cause precisely because it is its symbol. The liturgy of the world is expressed and made present in the Church's liturgy, and so the cosmic liturgy causes the Church's liturgy. But by manifesting the liturgy of the world, the Church's sacramental worship is the cause of the original liturgy. In this sense, the liturgy of the Church and the liturgy of the world depend upon each other for their completion.

If the sacramental liturgy of the Church is the real, symbolic manifestation of the liturgy of the world, then it must express both God's self-communication to us and our self-surrender to God. The original liturgy is a dialogue, and the incarnate Word fulfilled both the divine and the human sides of that dialogue. The two dynamics are inseparably and triumphantly united in Christ, and that unity is embodied in the liturgy of the Church. This synergy was generally overlooked in traditional sacramental theology, which emphasized the activity of God at the expense of our active participation.

Traditional definitions of a sacrament say that a sacrament is a sign that effects grace *ex opere operato*. This definition was usually taken to mean that grace is conferred on the recipient of the sacrament through the sacramental sign itself, and neither the

35. K. Rahner, *Foundations of Christian Faith*, 427–429.

merit (holiness) of the minister nor that of the recipient is caus-ally involved. This interpretation encouraged magical and mechanical understandings of the sacraments. It also devalued the active participation in faith (the *opus operantis*) of those who received the sacraments. Rahner attempts to present the self-communication of God in the sacrament (the *opus operatum*) in a way that relates it to the activity of the participants.[36]

The idea that sacraments confer grace *ex opere operato* does not simply mean that the sacraments work infallibly. The popular Catholic approach to this concept has usually reduced it to the idea that the sacraments have an almost physical certainty of ef-fect, meaning that we are not certain that God responds to our merely "subjective" acts of faith, but we can be positive that we will receive his grace in the sacraments. This popular under-standing is faulty on two scores. First, the infallible effect ascribed here to the sacraments is in fact, according to the Coun-cil of Trent, bound up with a condition—the disposition of the recipient (the *opus operantis*)—even though this condition is not precisely the cause of the effect of grace but merely the condition necessary for it. Trent says that if adults are to receive a sacra-ment fruitfully, they must have the right disposition; they must actively cooperate in the reception of the sacrament with faith and love. Therefore, the sacramental rite involves an element of uncertainty about the presence of grace and its efficacy. With a sacrament, the recipients know just as little (and just as much) as they do with a merely 'subjective" action performed in faith as to whether it has really given them God's grace. Second, this popular understanding is faulty because it does not adequately distinguish the sacraments from other moments of the efficacious word of God in the Church, which also have infallible effects. For example, we saw above that if sinners faithfully and lovingly accept the word of God proclaimed by the Church calling them to repentance, then the event of God's grace infallibly takes place in them.

The idea that sacraments confer grace *ex opere operato* does not simply mean that the sacraments produce grace in virtue of

36. K. Rahner, *The Church and the Sacraments*, 24–33.

Christ and without any merit on the part of the minister or the recipient. It is true that the sacraments do this. But all grace comes by the power and virtue of Christ, and there are non-sacramental occasions in which grace is given without any merit, as in the case of every prevenient grace. When we say that the sacraments confer grace *ex opere operato*, we must be saying something that is characteristic of the sacraments and only of the sacraments and not of the efficacious word of God in the Church in general. It means that sacraments effect grace because they are basic acts of the Church's self-realization, and that they do so in situations that are decisive for our individual salvation histories.[37]

This interpretation is rooted in the view of the Church as the primary sacrament of God's efficacious grace in Jesus Christ, which we have examined above. Salvation history entered into its final and irreversible phase through Jesus Christ because he is the presence of the victorious mercy of God. In Christ, God's grace is in the world in such a way that it can never be vanquished. Jesus Christ is the full symbol of the victorious mercy of God, the symbol that renders present what it symbolizes. The Church is the symbol that manifests and thereby effects at the · historical level the abiding, saving presence of Christ. So the Church is the primary sacrament of the grace of God, possessing what has been brought definitively into the world by Christ: the irreversible grace of God, which conquers the guilt of humanity.

It is of the very nature of the Church, therefore, to be the primary sacrament through which Christ manifests and effects his saving grace in the world. If this is the Church's nature, it must be able to realize its nature in its basic acts. Since the Church is an efficacious event of grace, those basic acts will also be events of grace. Such basic acts, however, can only be self-realizations of the Church if they are acts to which the Church is fully committed and in which it is fully engaged. And such basic acts of the Church can only share in its character as the primary sacrament of salvation if they meet individuals who are in situations decisive for their salvation. The Church can and does realize it-

37. K. Rahner, "What Is a Sacrament?" 144–145; and "The Word and the Eucharist," 270–272.

self in such basic acts, and these and only these are the sacraments. The sacraments and only the sacraments are the Church's basic acts of full self-realization as the primary, efficacious sacrament of salvation in situations that are decisive for the salvation of the individual.[38]

When we say that the sacraments confer grace *ex opere operato*, we mean that what is true in general about the Church as the primary sacrament is also true of the individual sacraments. It means that we can be confident that grace is manifested and effective in the sacraments because and in the manner in which Christ is active in them through the Church for the individual. A sacrament confers grace because it is an *opus operantis Christi in Ecclesia*. The idea that God's grace is conferred without the subjective merit of the minister or of the recipient of the sacrament is only a negative and secondary formulation of this insight.[39]

This means that our full and active participation in faith is an essential part of the sacramental event. As the irrevocable and absolute offer of God's grace, the Church encounters the individual who either accepts or rejects that offer. It is only if the recipient of the sacrament accepts the offer of grace (in the case of an adult) that the sacrament is clearly efficacious. Therefore, the sacraments are not magical rites. They do not coerce God but rather are God's free act upon us, and they are efficacious only to the extent that they meet our openness and freedom. If we do affirm God's offer of grace, that response also takes place by the power of God's grace. Our self-surrender to God is an essential part of worship as a sacramental event.[40]

The liturgy of the world is simultaneously a human achievement and a gift of God. While it is radically caused and sustained by God, it is nonetheless something we accomplish. The same synergy characterizes the liturgy of the Church. We are not called to be passive spectators at the Church's worship but to freely and fully enter into it. Our participation is an essential part of sacramental worship. Without it, the sacraments cannot be-

38. K. Rahner, *Foundations of Christian Faith*, 427–429.

39. K. Rahner, "The Word and the Eucharist," 372–378.

40. K. Rahner, *Foundations of Christian Faith*, 413–415; and "Personal and Sacramental Piety," 109–133.

come liturgy, and so they will not be events of grace. The more actively we participate in the liturgy of the Church, the more actively we will participate in that silent and secret liturgy, which is the deepest meaning of our lives. And then the entire universe will be transfigured in our communion with God.

Bibliography

PRIMARY SOURCES

Rahner, Karl. "The Abiding Significance of the Second Vatican Council." TI 20. New York: Crossroad (1981) 90-102. ("Die bleibende Bedeutung des II. Vatikanischen Konzils." STh 14. Einsiedeln: Benziger [1980] 303-318.)

_____. "Anonymous and Explicit Faith." TI 16. New York: Crossroad (1983) 52-59. ("Anonymen und expliziter Glaube." STh 12. Einsiedeln: Benziger [1975] 76-84.)

_____. "Anonymous Christians." TI 6. New York: Crossroad (1982) 390-398. ("Die anonymen Christen." STh 6. Einsiedeln: Benziger [1968] 545-554.)

_____. "Being Open to God as Ever Greater." TI 7. New York: Seabury (1977) 25-46. ("Vom Offensein für den je größern Gott." STh 7. Einsiedeln: Benziger [1966] 32-53.)

_____. "Ein Brief von P. Karl Rahner." *Der Mensch als Geheimnis: Die Anthropologie Karl Rahners*. Klaus Fischer. Freiburg: Herder (1974) 400-410.

_____. "The Christian Among Unbelieving Relations." TI 3. New York: Crossroad (1982) 355-372. ("Der Christ und siene ungläubigen Verwandten." STh 3. Einsiedeln: Benziger [1956] 419-448.)

_____. "Christian Dying." TI 18. New York: Crossroad (1983) 226-256. ("Das christliche Sterben." STh 13. Einsiedeln: Benziger [1978] 269-304.)

_____. "On Christian Dying." TI 7. New York: Seabury (1977) 285-293. ("Über das christliche Sterben." STh 7. Einsiedeln: Benziger [1966] 273-280.)

_____. "Christian Living Formerly and Today." TI 7. New York: Seabury (1977) 3-24. ("Frömmigkeit früher und heute." STh 7. Einsiedeln: Benziger [1966] 11-31.)

_____. "Christianity and the Non-Christian Religions." TI 5. New York: Crossroad (1983) 15-134. ("Das Christentum und die nichtchristlichen Religionen." STh 5. Einsiedeln: Benziger [1968] 136-158.)

_____. "Christmas in the Light of the Ignatian Exercises." TI 17. New York: Crossroad (1981) 3-7. ("Weihnacht im Licht der Exerzitien." STh 12. Einsiedeln: Benziger [1975] 329-334.)

_____. "Christmas, The Festival of Eternal Youth." TI 7. New York: Seabury (1977) 121-126. ("Weihnachten, Fest der ewigen Jugend." STh 7. Einsiedeln: Benziger [1966] 123-127.)

_____. "Christology in the Setting of Modern Man's Understanding of Himself and His World." TI 11. New York: Crossroad (1982) 215-229. ("Christologie im Rahmen des modernen Selbst- und Weltverständnisses." STh 9. Einsiedeln: Benziger [1970] 227-241.)

_____. "Christology Today?" TI 17. New York: Crossroad (1981) 24-38. ("Christologie heute?" STh 12. Einsiedeln: Benziger [1975] 353-369.)

_____. "Christology Within an Evolutionary View of the World." TI 5. New York: Crossroad (1983) 157-192. ("Die Christologie innerhalb einer evolutiven Weltanschauung." STh 5. Einsiedeln: Benziger [1968] 183-221.)

_____. The Church and the Sacraments. New York: Herder and Herder, 1963.

_____. "Church, Churches and Religions." TI 10. New York: Seabury (1977) 30-49. ("Kirche, Kirchen und Religionen." STh 8. Einsiedeln: Benziger [1967] 355-373.)

_____. "The Church's Redemptive Provenance from the Death and Resurrection of Jesus." TI 19. New York: Crossroad (1983) 24-38. ("Heilsgeschichtliche Herkunft der Kirche von Tod und Auferstehung Jesu." STh 14. Einsiedeln: Benziger [1980] 73-90.)

_____. "The Concept of Mystery in Catholic Theology." TI 4. New York: Crossroad (1982) 36-73. ("Über den Begriff des Geheimnisses in der katholischen Theologie." STh 4. Einsiedeln: Benziger [1967] 51-99.)

_____. "Concerning the Relationship Between Nature and Grace." TI 1. Baltimore: Helicon (1961) 297-317. ("Über das Verhältnis von Natur und Gnade." STh 1. Einsiedeln: Benziger [1954] 323-345.)

_____. "Considerations on the Active Role of the Person in the Sacramental Event." TI 14. New York: Seabury (1976) 161-184. ("Überlegungen zum personalen Vollzug des sakramentalen Geschehens." STh 10. Einsiedeln: Benziger [1972] 405-429.)

_____. "Courage for an Ecclesial Christianity." TI 20. New York: Crossroad (1981) 3-12. ("Vom Mut zum kirchlichen Christentum." STh 14. Einsiedeln: Benziger [1980] 11-22.)

_____. "Current Problems in Christology." TI 1. Baltimore: Helicon (1961) 149-200. ("Probleme der Christologie von heute." STh 1. Einsiedeln: Benziger [1967] 169-222.)

_____. "The Death of Jesus and the Closure of Revelation." TI 18. New York: Crossroad (1983) 132-142. ("Tod Jesu und Abgeschossenheit der Offenbarung." STh 13. Einsiedeln: Benziger [1978] 159-171.)

_____. "On the Diaconate." TI 12. New York: Seabury (1974) 61–80. ("Über den Diakonat." STh 9. Einsiedeln: Benziger [1970] 395–414.)

_____. "The Dignity and Freedom of Man." TI 2. Baltimore: Helicon (1963) 235–263. ("Würde und Freiheit des Menschen." STh 2. Einsiedeln: Benziger [1955] 247–277.)

_____. "Dogmatic Notes on 'Ecclesiological Piety.'" TI 5. New York: Cross-road (1983) 336–365. ("Dogmatische Randbemerkungen zur Kirchenfrömmig-keit." STh 5. Einsiedeln: Benziger [1968] 379–410.)

_____. "Dogmatic Questions on Easter." TI 4. New York: Crossroad (1982) 121–133. ("Dogmatische Fragen zur Osterfrömmigkeit." STh 4. Einsiedeln: Benziger [1960] 157–172.)

_____. "Dogmatic Reflections on the Knowledge and Self-consciousness of Christ." TI 5. New York: Crossroad (1983) 193–215. ("Dogmatische Er-wägungen über das Wissen und Selbstbewußtsein Christi." STh 5. Ein-siedeln: Benziger [1968] 222–245.)

_____. "On the Duration of the Presence of Christ After Communion." TI 4. New York: Crossroad (1982) 312–320. ("Über die Dauer der Gegenwart Christi nach dem Kommunionempfang." STh 4. Einsiedeln: Benziger [1960] 387–397.)

_____. "Encounters with the Risen Christ." TI 7. New York: Seabury (1977) 169–176. ("Begegnungen mit dem Auferstandenen." STh 7. Einsiedeln: Ben-ziger [1966] 166–173.)

_____. "The Eternal Significance of the Humanity of Jesus for Our Relation-ship with God." TI 3. New York: Crossroad (1982) 35–46. ("Die ewige Be-deutung der Menschheit Jesu für unser Gottesverhältnis." STh 3. Einsiedeln: Benziger [1967] 47–60.)

_____. "The Eucharist and Our Daily Lives." TI 7. New York: Seabury (1977) 211–226. ("Eucharistie und alltägliches Leben." STh 7. Einsiedeln: Benziger [1966] 204–220.)

_____. "The Eucharist and Suffering." TI 3. New York: Crossroad (1982) 161–170. ("Eucharistie und Leiden." STh 3. Einsiedeln: Benziger [1967] 191–202.)

_____. "Eucharistische Anbetung." STh 16. Einsiedeln: Benziger (1984) 300–304.

_____. "The Experience of God Today." TI 11. New York: Crossroad (1982) 149–165. ("Gotteserfahrung heute." STh 9. Einsiedeln: Benziger [1970] 161–176.)

_____. "Experience of Self and Experience of God." TI 13. New York:

161

Crossroad (1983) 122–132. ("Selbsterfahrung und Gotteserfahrung." STh 10. Einsiedeln: Benziger [1972] 133–144.)

———. "Experience of the Holy Spirit." TI 18. New York: Crossroad (1983) 189–210. ("Erfahrung des Heiligen Geistes." STh 13. Einsiedeln: Benziger [1978] 226–251.)

———. "Experience of the Spirit and Existential Commitment." TI 16. New York: Crossroad (1983) 24–34. ("Erfahrung des Geistes und existentielle Entscheidung." STh 12. Einsiedeln: Benziger [1975] 41–53.)

———. "Experience of Transcendence from the Standpoint of Catholic Dogmatics." TI 18. New York: Crossroad (1983) 173–188. ("Transzendenzerfahrung aus katholisch-dogmatischer Sicht." STh 13. Einsiedeln: Benziger [1978] 207–225.)

———. "Experiencing Easter." TI 7. New York: Seabury (1977) 159–168. ("Ostererfahrung." STh 7. Einsiedeln: Benziger [1966] 157–165.)

———. "The Festival of the Future of the World." TI 7. New York: Seabury (1977) 181–185. ("Fest der Zukunft der Welt." STh 7. Einsiedeln: Benziger [1966] 178–182.)

———. "Following the Crucified." TI 18. New York: Crossroad (1983) 157–170. ("Nachfolge des Gekreuzigten." STh 13. Einsiedeln: Benziger [1978] 188–203.)

———. "Forgotten Truths Concerning the Sacrament of Penance." TI 2. Baltimore: Helicon (1963) 135–174. ("Vergesene Wahrheiten über das Bußsakrament." STh 2. Einsiedeln: Benziger [1955] 143–184.)

———. Foundations of Christian Faith: An Introduction to the Idea of Christianity. New York: Seabury, 1978. (Grundkurs der Glaubens: Einführung in den Begriff des Christentums. Freiburg: Herder, 1984.)

———. "Fragen der Sakramententheologie." STh 16. Einsiedeln: Benziger (1984) 398–405.

———. "Freedom in the Church." TI 2. Baltimore: Helicon (1963) 89–107. ("Die Freiheit in der Kirche." STh 2. Einsiedeln: Benziger [1955] 95–114.)

———. "Glaube und Sakrament." STh 16. Einsiedeln: Benziger (1984) 387–397.

———. Grace in Freedom. New York: Herder and Herder, 1969.

———. " 'He Descended into Hell.' " TI 7. New York: Seabury (1977) 145–150. (" 'Abgestiegen ins Totenreich.' " STh 7. Einsiedeln: Benziger [1966] 145–149.)

———. " 'He Will Come Again.' " TI 7. New York: Seabury (1977) 177–180. ("Er wird wiederkommen." STh 7. Einsiedeln: Benziger [1966] 174–177.)

162

_____. *Hearers of the Word,* 1st ed. Trans. J. Donceel. Milwaukee: Marquette University Press, 1982. (*Hörer des Wortes: Zur Grundlegung einer Religions philosophie.* Hrsg. J. B. Metz. München: Kösel, 1963.)

_____. "Hidden Victory." TI 7. New York: Seabury (1977) 151–158. ("Verborgener Sieg." STh 7. Einsiedeln: Benziger [1966] 150–156.)

_____. "Hiddenness of God." TI 16. New York: Crossroad (1983) 227–243. ("Über die Verborgenheit Gottes." STh 12. Einsiedeln: Benziger [1975] 285–305.)

_____. "History of the World and Salvation-History." TI 5. New York: Crossroad (1983) 97–114. ("Weltgeschichte und Heilsgeschichte." STh 5. Einsiedeln: Benziger [1962] 115–135.)

_____. "Holy Night." TI 7. New York: Seabury (1977) 127–131. ("Heilige Nacht." STh 7. Einsiedeln: Benziger [1966] 128–132.)

_____. *Hominisation: The Evolutionary Origin of Man as a Theological Problem.* Freiburg: Herder, 1965. ("Die Hominisation als theologische Frage." *Das Problem der Hominisation.* K. Rahner und P. Overhage. Freiburg: Herder, 1958.)

_____. "How the Priest Should View His Official Ministry." TI 14. New York: Seabury (1976) 202–219. ("Zum Selbstverständnis des Amtspriesters." STh 10. Einsiedeln: Benziger [1972] 448–466.)

_____. "The Human Question of Meaning in Face of the Absolute Mystery of God." TI 18. New York: Crossroad (1983) 89–104. ("Die menschliche Sinnfrage vor dem absoluten Geheimnis Gottes." STh 13. Einsiedeln: Benziger [1978] 111–128.)

_____. " 'I Believe in Jesus Christ,' Interpreting an Article of Faith." TI 9. New York: Seabury (1977) 165–168. ("Ich glaube an Jesus Christus." STh 8. Einsiedeln: Benziger [1967] 213–217.)

_____. "Ideas for a Theology of Death," TI 13. New York: Crossroad (1983) 169–186. ("Zu einer Theologie des Todes." STh 10. Einsiedeln: Benziger [1972] 181–199.)

_____. "On the Importance of the Non-Christian Religions for Salvation." TI 18. New York: Crossroad (1983) 288–295. ("Über die Heilsbedeutung der nichtchristlichen Religionen." STh 13. Einsiedeln: Benziger [1978] 341–350.)

_____. "Introduction." *Apologetics and the Eclipse of Mystery: Mystagogy According to Karl Rahner.* James J. Bacik. Notre Dame: University of Notre Dame Press, 1980.

_____. "Introductory Observations on Thomas Aquinas' Theology of the Sacraments in General." TI 14. New York: Seabury (1976) 149–160. ("Einleitende Bemerkungen zur allgemeinen Sakramentenlehre bei Thomas von Aquin." STh 10. Einsiedeln: Benziger [1972] 392-404.)

_____. "An Investigation of the Incomprehensibility of God in St. Thomas Aquinas." TI 16. New York: Crossroad (1983) 244-254. ("Fragen zur Unbegreiflichkeit Gottes nach Thomas von Aquin." STh 12 Einsiedeln: Benziger [1975] 306-319.)

_____. "Jesus Christ in the Non-Christian Religions." TI 17. New York: Crossroad (1981) 39-50. ("Jesus Christus in den nichtchristlichen Religionen." STh 12. Einsiedeln: Benziger [1975] 370-383.)

_____. "Jesus' Resurrection." TI 17. New York: Crossroad (1981) 16-23. ("Jesu Auferstehung." STh 12. Einsiedeln: Benziger [1975] 344-352.)

_____. *Karl Rahner in Dialogue: Conversations and Interviews, 1965-1982.* Eds. P. Imhoff and Hubert Biallowons. Trans. ed. H. Egan. New York: Crossroad, 1986.

_____. "Marriage as a Sacrament." TI 10. New York: Seabury (1977) 199-221. ("Die Ehe als Sakrament." STh 8. Einsiedeln: Benziger [1967] 519-540.)

_____. "The Meaning of Frequent Confession of Devotion." TI 3. Baltimore: Helicon (1967) 177-189. ("Vom Sinn der häufigen Andachtsbeichte." STh 3. Einsiedeln: Benziger [1956] 211-226.)

_____. *Meditations on the Sacraments.* New York: Seabury, 1977.

_____. "Membership of the Church According to the Teaching of Pius XII's Encyclical 'Mystici Corporis Christi.' " TI 2. Baltimore: Helicon (1963) 1-88. ("Die Gliedschaft in der Kirche nach der Lehre der Enzyklika Pius' XII 'Mystici Corporis Christi.' " STh 2. Einsiedeln: Benziger [1968] 7-94.)

_____. "The Mystery of the Trinity." TI 16. New York: Crossroad (1983) 255-259. ("Um das Geheimnis der Dreifaltigkeit." STh 12. Einsiedeln: Benziger [1975] 320-325.)

_____. "Mystical Experience and Mystical Theology." TI 17. New York: Crossroad (1981) 90-99. ("Mystische Erfahrung und mystische Theologie." STh 12. Einsiedeln: Benziger [1975] 428-438.)

_____. "Nature and Grace." TI 4. New York: Crossroad (1982) 165-188. ("Natur und Gnade." STh 4. Einsiedeln: Benziger [1967] 209-236.)

_____. "Observations on the Concept of Revelation." *Revelation and Tradition.* K. Rahner and J. Ratzinger. Freiburg: Herder (1966) 9-25.

_____. "Observations on the Doctrine of God in Catholic Dogmatics." TI 9. New York: Seabury (1977) 127-144. ("Bemerkungen zur Gotteslehre in der katholischen Dogmatik." STh 8. Einsiedeln: Benziger [1967] 165–186.)

_____. "Observations on the Problem of the 'Anonymous Christian.' " TI 14. New York: Seabury (1976) 280–294. ("Bemerkungen zum Problem des 'anonymen Christen.' " STh 10. Einsiedeln: Benziger [1972] 531–546.)

_____. "The One Christ and the Universality of Salvation." TI 16. New York: Crossroad (1983) 199–224. ("Der eine Jesus Christus und die Universalität des Heils." STh 12. Einsiedeln: Benziger [1975] 251–282.)

_____. "The One Mediator and Many Mediations." TI 9. New York: Seabury (1977) 169–184. ("Der eine Mittler und die Vielfalt der Vermittlungen." STh 8. Einsiedeln: Benziger [1967] 218–235.)

_____. "Oneness and Threefoldness of God in Discussion with Islam." TI 18. New York: Crossroad (1983) 105–121. ("Einzigkeit und Dreifaltigkeit Gottes im Gespräch mit dem Islam." STh 13. Einsiedeln: Benziger [1978] 129–147.)

_____. "The Passion and Asceticism." TI 3. New York: Crossroad (1982) 58–85. ("Passion und Aszese." STh 3. Einsiedeln: Benziger [1956] 73–104.)

_____. "Peace on Earth." TI 7. New York: Seabury (1977) 132–135. ("Friede auf Erden." STh 7. Einsiedeln: Benziger [1966] 133–136.)

_____. "Penance as an Additional Act of Reconciliation with the Church." TI 10. New York: Seabury (1977) 125–149. ("Das Sakrament der Buße als Wiederversöhnung mit der Kirche." STh 8. Einsiedeln: Benziger [1967] 447–471.)

_____. Penance in the Early Church. TI 15. New York: Crossroad, 1982. (Frühe Bussgeschichte in Einzeluntersuchen. STh 11. Einsiedeln: Benziger, 1973.)

_____. "Personal and Sacramental Piety." TI 2. Baltimore: Helicon (1966) 109–131. ("Personale und sakramentale Frömmigkeit." STh 2. Einsiedeln: Benziger [1968] 115–141.)

_____. "The Point of Departure in Theology for Determining the Nature of the Priestly Office." TI 12. New York: Seabury (1974) 31–38. ("Der theologische Ansatzpunkt für die Bestimmung des Wesens des Amtspriestertums." STh 9. Einsiedeln: Benziger [1970] 366–372.)

_____. "The Position of Christology in the Church Between Exegesis and Dogmatics." TI 11. New York: Crossroad (1982) 185–214. ("Kirchliche Christologie zwischen Exegese und Dogmatik." STh 9. Einsiedeln: Benziger [1970] 197–226.)

_____. "The Possibility and Necessity of Prayer." Christian at the Crossroads. New York: Seabury (1975) 48–61.

_____. "The Prayer of the Individual and the Liturgy of the Church." *Grace in Freedom.* New York: Herder and Herder (1969) 137–181.

_____. "On the Presence of Christ in the Diaspora Community According to the Teaching of the Second Vatican Council." TI 10. New York: Seabury (1977) 84–102. ("Über die Gegenwart Christi in der Diasporagemeinde nach der Lehre des Zweiten Vatikanischen Konzils." STh 8. Einsiedeln: Benziger [1967] 409–425.)

_____. "The Presence of Christ in the Sacrament of the Lord's Supper." TI 4. New York: Crossroad (1982) 287–311. ("Die Gegenwart Christi im Sakrament des Herrenmahles." STh 4. Einsiedeln: Benziger, [1960] 357–386.)

_____. "The Presence of the Lord in the Christian Community at Worship." TI 10. New York: Seabury (1977) 71–83. ("Die Gegenwart des Herren in der christlichen Kultgemeinde." STh 8. Einsiedeln: Benziger [1967] 395–408.)

_____. "Problems Concerning Confession." TI 3. Baltimore: Helicon (1967) 190–206. ("Beichtprobleme." STh 3. Einsiedeln: Benziger [1956] 227–245.)

_____. "The Quest for Approaches Leading to an Understanding of the Mystery of the God–Man Jesus." TI 13. New York: Crossroad (1983) 195-200. ("Auf der Suche nach Zugängen zum Verständnis des gottmenschlichen Geheimnisses Jesu." STh 10. Einsiedeln: Benziger [1972] 209–214.)

_____. "Reflections on Methodology in Theology." TI 11. New York: Crossroad (1982) 68–114. ("Überlegungen zur Methode der Theologie." STh 9. Einsiedeln: Benziger [1970] 79–126.)

_____. "Reflections on the Experience of Grace." TI 3. New York: Crossroad (1982) 86–90. ("Über die Erfahrung der Gnade." STh 3. Einsiedeln: Benziger [1967] 105–110.)

_____. "Religious Feeling Inside and Outside the Church." TI 17. New York: Crossroad (1981) 228–242. ("Kirchliche und außerkirchliche Religiosität." STh 12. Einsiedeln: Benziger [1975] 582–598.)

_____. "Remarks on the Dogmatic Treatise 'De Trinitate.'" TI 4. New York: Crossroad (1982) 77–102. ("Bemerkungen zum dogmatischen Traktat 'De Trinitate.'" STh 4. Einsiedeln: Benziger [1967] 103–133.)

_____. "Remarks on the Importance of the History of Jesus for Catholic Dogmatics." TI 13. New York: Crossroad (1983) 201–212. ("Bemerkungen zur Bedeutung der Geschichte Jesu für die katholische Dogmatik." STh 10. Einsiedeln: Benziger [1972] 215–226.)

_____. "The Sacramental Basis for the Role of the Layman in the Church." TI 8. New York: Seabury (1977) 51–74. ("Sakramentale Grundlegung des Laienstandes in der Kirche." STh 7. Einsiedeln: Benziger [1966] 330–350.)

_____. "The Scandal of Death." TI 7. New York: Seabury (1977) 140–144. ("Das Ärgernis des Todes." STh 7. Einsiedeln: Benziger [1966] 141–144.)

_____. "The Secret of Life." TI 6. New York: Crossroad (1982) 141–152. ("Vom Geheimnis des Lebens." STh 6. Einsiedeln: Benziger [1968] 171–184.)

_____. "See, What a Man!" TI 7. New York: Seabury (1977) 136–139. ("Seht, welch ein Mensch." STh 7. Einsiedeln: Benziger [1966] 137–140.)

_____. "The Significance in Redemptive History of the Individual Member of the Church." The Christian Commitment: Essays in Pastoral Theology. New York: Sheed and Ward (1963) 75–113.

_____. "Some Implications of the Scholastic Concept of Uncreated Grace." TI 1. Baltimore: Helicon, (1961) 319–346. ("Zu scholastischen Begrifflichkeit der ungeschaffenen Gnade." STh 1. Einsiedeln: Benziger [1954] 347–375.)

_____. Spirit in the World. Montreal: Palm Publishers, 1968. (Geist in Welt: Zur Metaphysik der Endlichen Erkenntnis bei Thomas von Aquin. Hrsg. J. B. Metz. München: Kösel, 1957.)

_____. Spiritual Exercises. London: Sheed and Ward, 1966.

_____. "On the Spirituality of the Easter Faith." TI 17. New York: Crossroad (1981) 8–15. ("Über die Spiritualität des Osterglaubens." STh 12. Einsiedeln: Benziger [1975] 335–343.)

_____. "Taufe und Tauferneuerung." STh 16. Einsiedeln: Benziger (1984) 406–417.

_____. "Theological Considerations on the Moment of Death." TI 11. New York: Crossroad (1982) 309–321. ("Theologische Erwägungen über den Eintritt des Todes." STh 9. Einsiedeln: Benziger [1970] 323–335.)

_____. "The Theological Dimension of the Question About Man." TI 17. New York: Crossroad (1981) 53–70. ("Die theologische Dimension der Frage nach dem Menschen." STh 12. Einsiedeln: Benziger [1975] 387–406.)

_____. "Theological Observations on the Concept of Time." TI 11. New York: Crossroad (1982) 288–308. ("Theologische Bemerkungen zum Zeitbegriff." STh 9. Einsiedeln: Benziger [1970] 302–322.)

_____. "Theology and Anthropology." TI 9. New York: Seabury (1977) 28–45. ("Theologie und Anthropologie." STh 8. Einsiedeln: Benziger [1967] 43–65.)

_____. On the Theology of Death. Montreal: Palm Publishers, 1961. (Zur Theologie des Todes. Freiburg: Herder, 1961.)

_____. "Theology of Freedom." TI 6. New York: Crossroad (1982) 178–196. ("Theologie der Freiheit." STh 6. Einsiedeln: Benziger [1968] 215–237.)

_____. "On the Theology of Freedom." *Freedom and Man.* Ed. J. C. Murray. New York: Kenedy (1965) 201–217.

_____. "On the Theology of the Incarnation." TI 4. New York: Crossroad (1982) 105–120. ("Zur Theologie der Menschwerdung." STh 4. Einsiedeln: Benziger [1960] 137–155.)

_____. "The Theology of the Symbol." TI 4. Baltimore: Helicon (1966) 221–252. ("Zur Theologie des Symbols." STh 4. Einsiedeln: Benziger [1960] 275–311.)

_____. "On the Theology of Worship." TI 19. New York: Crossroad (1983) 141–149. ("Zur Theologie des Gottesdienstes." STh 14. Einsiedeln: Benziger [1980] 227–237.)

_____. *Theos* in the New Testament." TI 1. Baltimore: Helicon (1961) 79–148. ("Theos im Neuen Testament." STh 1. Einsiedeln: Benziger [1954] 91–167.)

_____. "Thoughts on the Theology of Christmas." TI 3. New York: Crossroad (1982) 24–34. ("Zur Theologie der Weihnachtsfeier." STh 3. Einsiedeln: Benziger [1956] 35–46.)

_____. *The Trinity.* New York: Seabury, 1974.

_____. "The Two Basic Types of Christology." TI 13. New York: Crossroad (1983) 213–223. ("Die zwei Grundtypen der Christologie." STh 10. Einsiedeln: Benziger [1972] 227–238.)

_____. "The Unity of Spirit and Matter in the Christian Understanding of Faith." TI 6. New York: Crossroad (1982) 153–177. ("Die Einheit von Geist und Materie im Christlichen Glaubensverständnis." STh 6. Einsiedeln: Benziger [1968] 185–214.)

_____. *Watch and Pray with Me: The Seven Last Words.* New York: Seabury, 1966.

_____. "What Does It Mean Today to Believe in Jesus Christ?" TI 18. New York: Crossroad (1983) 143–156. ("Was heißt heute an Jesus Christus glauben?" STh 13. Einsiedeln: Benziger [1978] 172–187.)

_____. "What Is a Sacrament?" TI 14. New York: Seabury (1976) 135–148. ("Was ist ein Sakrament?" STh 10. Einsiedeln: Benziger [1972] 377–391.)

_____. "What Is Man?" *Christian at the Crossroads.* New York: Seabury (1975) 11–20.

_____. "The Word and the Eucharist." TI 4. Baltimore: Helicon (1966) 253–286. ("Wort und Eucharistie." STh 4. Einsiedeln: Benziger [1960] 313–355.)

_____. "Zur Situation des Bußsakramentes." STh 16. Einsiedeln: Benziger (1984) 418–437.

_____, ed. *Encyclopedia of Theology: The Concise* Sacramentum Mundi. New York: Crossroad, 1982.

Rahner, Karl and A. Haussling. *The Celebration of the Eucharist.* New York: Herder and Herder, 1968.

Rahner, Karl and H. Vorgrimler. *Dictionary of Theology,* 2nd ed. New York: Crossroad, 1981. (*Kleines Theologisches Wörterbuch.* Freiburg: Herder, 1976.)

Rahner, Karl und J. Höfer, hrsg. *Lexikon für Theologie und Kirche.* Freiburg: Herder, 1959.

SECONDARY SOURCES

Allik, Tiina. "Karl Rahner on Materiality and Human Knowledge." Thomist 49 (1985) 357–386.

Bacik, James J. *Apologetics and the Eclipse of Mystery: Mystagogy According to Karl Rahner.* Notre Dame: University of Notre Dame Press, 1980.

Beggiani, Seely. "A Case for Logocentric Theology." TS 32 (1971) 371–406.

Bent, Charles N. "Some Critical Reflections on Karl Rahner's Thesis Concerning Man as a Hearer of the Word." Word in the World. Ed. R. J. Clifford and G. W. McRae. Cambridge, Mass.: Weston College Press (1973) 209–220.

Bradley, Denis. "Rahner's *Spirit in the World:* Aquinas or Hegel?" Thomist 41 (1977) 167–199.

_____. "Religious Faith and the Mediation of Being: The Hegelian Dilemma in Rahner's *Hearers of the Word.*" Modern Schoolman 55 (1978) 127–146.

Breuning, Wilhelm. "Zum Verhältnis von Wort und Sakrament." *Glaube im Prozess: Christsein nach dem II. Vatikanum, Für Karl Rahner.* Hrsg. E. Klinger und K. Wittstadt. Freiburg: Herder (1984) 418–430.

Buckley, James J. "On Being a Symbol: An Appraisal of Rahner." TS 40 (1979) 453–473.

Callahan, C. Annice. "Karl Rahner's Theology of Symbol: Basis for His Theology of the Church and the Sacraments." Irish Theological Quarterly 49 (1982) 195–205.

Canlas, Florentino M. "Darkness or Light: Rahner and Collopy on the Theology of Death," Bijdragen 45 (1984) 251–275, 384–416.

Carmody, Denise Lardner and John T. Carmody. "Christology in Karl Rahner's Evolutionary World View." Religion in Life 49 (1980) 195–210.

Carr, Anne. "The God Who Is Involved." *Theology Today* 38 (1981) 314–328.

_____. *The Theological Method of Karl Rahner.* Missoula: Scholar's Press, 1977.

Cawte, John. "Karl Rahner's Conception of God's Self-Communication to Man." *Heythrop Journal* 25 (1984) 260–271.

Chandlee, H. Ellsworth. "The Liturgical Movement." *The New Westminster Dictionary of Liturgy and Worship.* Ed. J. G. Davies. Philadelphia: Westminster Press (1986) 307–314.

Collopy, Bartholomew J. "Theology and the Darkness of Death." *Theological Studies* 39 (1978) 22–54.

Donceel, Joseph. "Causality and Evolution: A Survey of Some Neo-Scholastic Theories." *New Scholasticism* 39 (1965) 295–315.

_____. "Second Thoughts on the Nature of God." *Thought* 46 (1971) 346–370.

Dych, William V. "The Achievement of Karl Rahner." TD 31 (1984) 325–333.

_____. "Method in Theology According to Karl Rahner." *Theology and Discovery: Essays in Honor of Karl Rahner, S.J.* Ed. W. J. Kelly. Milwaukee: Marquette University Press (1980) 39–53.

Eberhard, Kenneth D. "Karl Rahner and the Supernatural Existential." *Thought* 46 (1971) 537–561.

Edwards, Denis. "Experience of God and Explicit Faith: A Comparison of John of the Cross and Karl Rahner." *Thomist* 46 (1982) 33–74.

Egan, Harvey. "The Devout Christian of the Future Will . . . Be a 'Mystic.' Mysticism and Karl Rahner's Theology." *Theology and Discovery: Essays in Honor of Karl Rahner, S.J.* Ed. W. J. Kelly. Milwaukee: Marquette University Press (1980) 139–158.

_____. *What Are They Saying About Mysticism?* New York: Paulist, 1982.

Eicher, Peter. *Die anthropologische Wende. K. Rahners philosophischer Weg vom Wesen des Menschen zur personalen Existenz.* Freiburg: Universitätsverlag, 1970.

Falk, Heinrick. "Can Spirit Come from Matter?" *International Philosophical Quarterly* 7 (1967) 541–555.

Fahey, Michael A. "1904–1984, Karl Rahner, Theologian." PCTSA 39 (1984) 84–98.

Fiorenza, Francis Schüssler. "Seminar on Rahner's Ecclesiology: Jesus and the Foundations of the Church—An Analysis of the Hermeneutical Issues." *PCTSA* 33 (1978) 229–254.

Fischer, Klaus. *Gotteserfahrung: Mystagogie in der Theologie Karl Rahners und in der Theologie der Befreiung*. Mainz: Matthias-Grünewald Verlag, 1986.

_____. "Kritik der 'Grundpositionen'? Kritische Anmerkungen zu. B. van der Heijdens Buch über Karl Rahner." ZKTh 99 (1977) 74–89.

_____. *Der Mensch als Geheimnis: Die Anthropologie Karl Rahners*. Freiburg: Herder, 1974.

_____. "Wo der Mensch an das Geheimnis grenzt. Die mystagogische Struktur der Theologie Karl Rahners." ZKTh 98 (1976) 159–170.

Galvin, John P. "Jesus' Approach to Death: An Examination of Some Recent Studies." TS 41 (1980) 713–744.

_____. "The Resurrection of Jesus in Contemporary Catholic Systematics." *Heythrop Journal* 20 (1979) 123–145.

Greiner, Friedermann. "Die Menschlichkeit der Offenbarung. Die transzendentale Grundlegung der Theologie bei K. Rahner im Lichte seiner Christologie." ZKTh 100 (1978) 596–619.

Haught, John F. "What Is Logocentric Theology?" TS 33 (1972) 120–132.

Heijden, Bert van der. *Karl Rahner: Darstellung und Kritik seiner Grundposition*. Einsiedeln: Johannes Verlag, 1973.

Hill, William J. "Uncreated Grace: A Critique of Karl Rahner." *Thomist* 27 (1963) 333–356.

Honner, John. "Disclosed and Transcendental: Rahner and Ramsey on the Foundations of Theology." *Heythrop Journal* 22 (1981) 149–161.

_____. "Unity-in-Difference: Karl Rahner and Niels Bohr." TS 46 (1985) 480–506.

Hoye, William J. "A Critical Remark on Karl Rahner's *Hearers of the Word*." *Antonianum* 48 (1973) 508–532.

_____. *Die Verfinsterung des Absoluten Geheimnisses. Eine Kritik der Gotteslehre Karl Rahners*. Düsseldorf: Patmos, 1979.

Hünermann, Peter. "Reflexionen zum Sakramentenbegriff des II Vatikanums." *Glaube in Prozess: Christsein nach dem II. Vatikanum, Für Karl Rahner*. Hrsg. E. Klinger und K. Wittstadt. Freiburg: Herder (1984) 309–324.

Hurd, Robert L. "The Concept of Freedom in Rahner." *Listening* 17 (1982) 138–152.

Imhof, Paul und Hubert Biallowons, hrsg. *Karl Rahner: Bilder eines Lebens*. Köln: Benziger, 1985.

Inbody, Tyron. "Rahner's Christology: A Critical Assessment." *St. Luke's Journal of Theology* 25 (1982) 294–310.

Jüngel, Eberhard. "Das Verhältnis von ökonomischer und immanenter Trinität." ZThK 72 (1975) 353–364.

Kasper, Walter. "Die Kirche als universales Sakrament des Heils." *Glaube in Prozess: Christsein nach dèm II. Vatikanum, Für Karl Rahner.* Hrsg. E. Klinger und K. Wittstadt. Freiburg: Herder (1984) 221–239.

————. *The God of Jesus Christ.* New York: Crossroad, 1984.

Kantzenbach, Friedrich W. "Die ekklesiologische Begründung des Heils der Nichtchristen." *Oecumencia* (1967) 210–234.

King, J. Norman. "The Experience of God in the Theology of Karl Rahner." *Thought* 53 (1978) 174–202.

————. *The God of Forgiveness and Healing in the Theology of Karl Rahner.* Lanham, Md.: University Press of America, 1982.

Knoch, Wendelin. "Das Heil des Menschen in seiner ekklesiologischen Dimension." *Wagnis Theologie: Erfahrungen mit der Theologie Karl Rahners.* Hrsg. H. Vorgrimler. Freiburg: Herder (1979) 487–498.

Koch, Traugott. "Natur und Gnade. Zur neueren Diskussion." KuD 16 (1970) 171–187.

Köhnlein, Manfred. *Was bringt das Sakrament? Disputation mit Karl Rahner.* Göttingen, 1971.

Künzle, Pius. "Sakramente und Ursakramente." FZPhTh 10 (1963) 428–444.

LaCunga, Catherine M. "Re-conceiving the Trinity as the Mystery of Salvation." *Scottish Journal of Theology* 38 (1985) 1–23.

Letter, P. de. " 'Pure' or 'Quasi'-Formal Causality." *Irish Theological Quarterly* 30 (1963) 36–47.

Linbeck, George A. "Sacramentality of the Ministry: Karl Rahner and a Protestant View." *Oecumencia* (1967) 282–301.

MacQuarrie, John. "The Anthropological Approach to Theology." *Heythrop Journal* 25 (1984) 272–287.

Maldonado, Luis. "Wort und Sakrament in der neueren Entwicklung der Pastoral." *Wagnis Theologie: Erfahrungen mit der Theologie Karl Rahners.* Hrsg. H. Vorgrimler. Freiburg: Herder (1979) 393–401.

Mawhinney, John J. "The Concept of Mystery in Karl Rahner's Philosophical Theology." *Union Seminary Quarterly Review* 24 (1968) 17–30.

McCool, Gerald A. "Person and Community in Karl Rahner." *Person and Community.* Ed. R. J. Roth. New York: Fordham University Press (1975) 63–86.

_____. "The Philosophical Theology of Rahner and Lonergan." *God Knowable and Unknowable.* Ed. R. J. Roth. New York: Fordham University Press (1973) 123–157.

_____. "The Philosophy of the Human Person in Karl Rahner's Theology." TS 22 (1961) 537–562.

McDermott, Brian O. "Roman Catholic Christology: Two Recurring Themes." TS 41 (1980) 334–367.

McManus, Fredrick R. "The Sacred Liturgy: Tradition and Change." *Remembering the Future: Vatican II and Tomorrow's Liturgical Agenda.* Ed. C. Last. New York: Paulist (1983) 11–32.

Metz, Johann B. "Freedom as a Threshold Problem Between Philosophy and Theology." *Philosophy Today* 10 (1966) 264–279.

_____. *Faith in History and Society.* New York: Crossroad, 1980.

Molnar, Paul D. "Can We Know God Directly? Rahner's Solution from Experience." TS 46 (1985) 228–261.

Moloney, Robert. "Seeing and Knowing: Some Reflections on Karl Rahner's Theory of Knowledge." *Heythrop Journal* 18 (1977) 399–419.

Motherway, Thomas J. "Supernatural Existential." *Chicago Studies* 4 (1965) 79–103.

Muck, Otto. *The Transcendental Method.* New York: Herder and Herder, 1968.

Mügge, Marlies. "Entwicklung und theologischer Kontext der Bußtheologie Karl Rahners." *Wagnis Theologie: Erfahrungen mit der Theologie Karl Rahners.* Hrsg. H. Vorgrimler. Freiburg: Herder (1979) 435–450.

Neumann, Karl. "Diasporakirche als sacramentum mundi. Karl Rahner und die Diskussion um Volkskirche—Gemeindekirche." *Trierer theologische Zeitschrift* 91 (1982) 52–71.

O'Donovan, Leo J. "A Journey into Time: The Legacy of Karl Rahner's Last Years." TS 46 (1985) 621–646.

_____. "Orthopraxis and Theological Method in Karl Rahner." PCTSA 35 (1980) 47–65.

_____, ed. "A Changing Ecclesiology in a Changing Church: A Symposium on Development in the Ecclesiology of Karl Rahner." TS 38 (1977) 736–762.

_____, ed. *A World of Grace: An Introduction to the Themes and Foundations of Karl Rahner's Theology.* New York: Seabury, 1980.

Ohlig, Karl-Heinz. "Impulse zu einer 'Christologie von unten' bei Karl Rahner." *Wagnis Theologie: Erfahrungen mit der Theologie Karl Rahners.* Hrsg. H. Vorgrimler. Freiburg: Herder (1979) 259–273.

Peter, Carl J. "The Position of Karl Rahner Regarding the Supernatural: A Comparative Study of Nature and Grace." PCTSA 20 (1965) 81–94.

_____. "A Shift to the Human Subject in Roman Catholic Theology." *Communio* (U.S.) 6 (1979) 56–72.

Pissarek-Hudelist, Herlinde. "Die Bedeutung der Sakramententheologie Karl Rahners für die Diskussion um das Priestertum der Frau." *Wagnis Theologie: Erfahrungen mit der Theologie Karl Rahners.* Hrsg. H. Vorgrimler. Freiburg: Herder (1979) 417–434.

Puntel, L. Bruno. "Zu den Begriffen 'transzendental' und 'kategorial' bei Karl Rahner." *Wagnis Theologie: Erfahrungen mit der Theologie Karl Rahners.* Hrsg. H. Vorgrimler. Freiburg: Herder (1979) 189–198.

Riesenhuber, Klaus. "Rahner's 'Anonymous Christian.' " *Christian Witness in the Secular City.* Ed. E. J. Morgan. Chicago: Loyola University Press (1970) 142–154.

Robertson, John C. "Rahner and Ogden: Man's Knowledge of God." *Harvard Theological Review* 63 (1970) 377–407.

Rolwing, Richard J. *A Philosophy of Revelation According to Karl Rahner.* Washington: University Press of America, 1978.

Schoonenberg, Piet. "Zur Trinitätslehre Karl Rahners." *Glaube im Prozess: Christsein nach dem II. Vatikanum, Für Karl Rahner.* Hrsg. E. Klinger und K. Wittstadt. Freiburg: Herder (1984) 471–491.

Schrofner, Erich. "Gnade und Erfahrung bei Karl Rahner und Leonardo Boff. Zwei Wege gegenwärtiger Gnadentheologie." *Geist und Leben* 53 (1980) 266–280.

Schulz, Hans-Joachim. "Karl Rahners Sakramententheologie: Zugang zu Ostkirche und ökumene." *Wagnis Theologie: Erfahrungen mit der Theologie Karl Rahners.* Hrsg. H. Vorgrimler. Freiburg: Herder (1979) 402–416.

Sica, Joseph F. *God So Loved the World.* Washington: University Press of America, 1981.

Skelley, Michael. "The Liturgy of the World and the Liturgy of the Church: Karl Rahner's Idea of Worship." *Worship* 63 (1989) 112–132.

Speck, Josef. *Karl Rahners theologische Anthropologie. Eine Einführung.* München: Kösel, 1967.

Spindeler, Alois. "Kirche und Sakramente. Ein Beitrag zur Diskussion mit Karl Rahner im Blick auf das Tridentinum." ThGl 53 (1963) 1-15.

Tallon, Andrew. *Personal Becoming: Karl Rahner's Christian Anthropology.* Milwaukee: Marquette University Press, 1982. (Also in *Thomist* 43 [1979] 7-177.)

_____. "Rahner and Personization." *Philosophy Today* 14 (1970) 44-56.

_____. "Spirit, Freedom, History: Karl Rahner's *Hörer des Wortes.*" *Thomist* 38 (1974) 908-936.

_____. "Spirit, Matter, Becoming. Karl Rahner's *Spirit in the World (Geist in Welt).*" *Modern Schoolman* 48 (1971) 151-165.

Tappeiner, Daniel A. "Sacramental Causality in Aquinas and Rahner." *Scottish Journal of Theology* 28 (1975) 243-258.

Taylor, Mark Lloyd. *God is Love: A Study in the Theology of Karl Rahner.* Atlanta: Scholars Press, 1986.

Vass, George. *The Mystery of Man and the Foundations of a Theological System: Understanding Karl Rahner,* Vol. II. London: Sheed and Ward, 1985.

_____. *A Theologian in Search of a Philosophy: Understanding Karl Rahner,* Vol I. London: Sheed and Ward, 1985.

Vorgrimler, Herbert. "Der Begriff der Selbsttranzendenz in der Theologie Karl Rahners." *Wagnis Theologie: Erfahrungen mit der Theologie Karl Rahners.* Hrsg. H. Vorgrimler. Freiburg: Herder (1979) 242-258.

_____. "Gotteserfahrung im Alltag. Der Beitrag Karl Rahners zu Spiritualität und Mystik." *Vor dem Geheimnis Gottes den Menschen verstehen. Karl Rahner zum 80. Geburtstag.* Hrsg. K. Lehman. München: Verlag Schnell und Steiner (1984) 62-78.

_____. "Karl Rahner: The Theologian's Contribution." *Vatican II Revisited: By Those Who Were There.* Ed. A. Stacpoole. Minneapolis: Winston Press, 1986, 32-46.

_____. *Understanding Karl Rahner: An Introduction to His Life and Thought.* New York: Crossroad, 1986.

Weger, Karl-Heinz. *Karl Rahner: An Introduction to His Theology.* New York: Seabury, 1980.

_____. "Überlegungen zum 'anonymen Christentum.' " *Wagnis Theologie: Erfahrungen mit der Theologie Karl Rahners.* Freiburg: Herder, 1979, 499-510.

Web, Paul. "Wie kann der Mensch Gott erfahren? Eine Überlegung zur Theologie Karl Rahners." *Theologisches Jahrbuch* (1982) 64-69. (Also in: ZKTh 102 [1980] 343-48.)

Yearley, Lee H. "Karl Rahner on the Relation of Nature and Grace." *Canadian Journal of Theology* 16 (1970) 219-31.